THINGS DO GO
Eddie, Gene and the

Spencer Leigh
Illustrations by John Firminger

Published by Finbarr International

ISBN 0-9529500-7-3

Finbarr International, Folkestone, Kent, CT20 2QQ

THINGS DO GO WRONG
Eddie, Gene and the UK Tour

CONTENTS

EDDIE COCHRAN

(back in the hit parade with 'Somethin' Else')

writes 'MY FONDEST WISH IS TO VISIT BRITAIN'

New picture of EDDIE

I GUESS my love for music dates back even further than I can remember. At least, that's what my family tells me. I am the youngest of five children. My two brothers and two sisters tell me they used to put me to sleep, when I was a baby, with the phonograph. The magic records were "Hot Pretzels" and " Beer Barrel Polka."

None of my family are in the entertainment business, but all of them have always had a love for music. They have helped and encouraged me in every way possible with my career since I first started.

I was born October 3, 1938, in Oklahoma City, Oklahoma. We moved to Albert Lea, Minnesota, while I was still a baby. I grew up there and I don't think anyone ever had a more wonderful childhood than I had.

Minnesota is a hunter's and fisherman's paradise, and my father indulged in both of these and took us along with him. That's where I get my liking for guns and hunting and all outdoor sports.

It was on one of my hunting trips that my brother shot me in the leg.

We were hunting, of all things, frogs. My brother had an automatic "22" and it had refused to fire. He was trying to work the lever and it went off accidentally and shot me in the leg.

I was in bed for several months, but I still like guns, of which I have quite a few, and still go on hunting trips.

First guitar

I got my first guitar when I was ten years old. Not long after that we moved to California, and as I did not know anyone, I turned to my guitar for companionship. I really started to play in earnest then.

It was at this time I met Connie " Guybo " Smith, my bass player. We started with several more boys playing for community affairs. I remember our first paid engagement. It was for the "Town Hall" employees of South Gate, California, in the South Gate Auditorium.

I say I remember, for I was rather nervous and lost my guitar pick several times—and also my voice was just changing and it cracked several times, much to my embarrassment !

Then I heard this new music with a beat that we know as rock 'n' roll, and I knew this was for me ! I started singing this music and I think it's the greatest !

It's music from the heart and that's the way I sing it. I feel it is here to stay with us maybe in a modified form, but in truth it has been with us for a long time in rhythm 'n' blues, and other forms of music.

Film break

About this time I met Jerry Capehart at a record session on which I was playing and he introduced me to Si Waronker, of Liberty Records. They arranged an audition for me and Mr. Waronker signed me to a contract.

When 20th Century-Fox asked me to appear in their picture of " The Girl Can't Help It," I got my first big break in pictures.

Soon after that Warner Brothers asked me to appear in their movie " Untamed Youth." A few months ago I just finished working in a picture for Hal Roach Studios called " Johnny Melody," which has not been released yet.

I enjoy acting very much and I hope some day to be a really great actor.

My first record release was " Sittin' In The Balcony." Much to my surprise the public liked it and even in England they seemed to like it, too.

I guess every entertainer has a dream of being able to go to England to perform, but it wasn't until my records of " Summertime Blues " and " C'mon Everybody " were released there that they asked for me.

I am so grateful to the British people for being so kind to me.

My fondest wish is to go to Britain. I planned a holiday there last summer, but I was too busy. I'll make it yet—and then I'll meet some of those kind people who have written me the best letters I've ever had.

On tour (below) in Denver, Colorado November '57

(Above) Eddie with Guybo Smith on Town Hall Party TV show

It's sure fine lookin' man, its something' else

Below Gene Vincent Record Date album that Eddie guested on

GENE VINCENT
Britain made me a professional

I HAVE travelled all over the world as a rock 'n' roll singer, but I tell you this: It has taken me these five months in Britain to become a real professional.

Too many visiting American singers come to this country thinking they know it all. But they don't.

And I'm the first to admit I still have a lot to learn.

This visit to England—which ends late in August—has been a real experience. I feel, too, it has been a great success.

But don't think I have made it a success on my own. I haven't. I owe a lot to Jack Good. That man has more musical sense in his little finger than I could acquire in a lifetime.

I am a very shy person—although many may not realise it. I always have been shy. Facing an audience used to terrify me.

In America I was just an amateur

Jack, however, has given me confidence.

For the first time I can look an audience straight in the face. But I used to sing just for the band and —don't laugh—myself!

However, one thing you may have noticed is, I never speak on the stage. This is something I can't do.

I don't know how to put my feelings into words. I'm not sure what to say. And if I do say something I think that people will find me very dull. A bore!

My rule is: Keep my mouth shut.

Of course, I would like to let the audience know how grateful I am for their applause and support. But I remain silent because I'd probably goof—or dry up.

While I've been in this country I've watched a bit of television and I must say the presentation of your shows is a hundred per cent better than shows on American TV.

For example, on our TV programme "American Bandstand," you're just put in front of a camera and told to get on with it. Also singing "live" in Britain is much better than miming to records which is the general rule in the States.

I enjoy meeting and working with some of your rock 'n' roll boys. But I can't say I agree with their habit of practising all the moves for their act *before* they go on stage. This, I feel, is all wrong.

When I get to work my moves are spontaneous. They're not rehearsed or worked out beforehand. That's one big difference between us.

When rock 'n' roll first came out in America the critics said it would last, at the most, six months. The time went by, then they gave it a further six. Now they don't say a word. And very wise they are, too.

I was interested to note that many people who slammed it in the early days—were the first to jump on the band-wagon when its popularity increased.

There are still those who look on rock 'n' roll as a crazy mixed-up trend that will pass. But they should remember that rock 'n' roll is still music.

I'm often asked what music I like best. Well, I like all types. I think people in the profession should. However, I must say that I don't rave about jazz. Perhaps that's because I don't understand it. If I had more opportunity of hearing it I might change my mind.

My real love is the blues. I was raised on it in Virginia where I was born.

I still remember, as a small boy, listening to the coloured folk singing "All God's Chil'n Got Shoes" as they went on their way to the cotton fields.

I sing blues numbers very often in the States.

I'm on the mailing list of most of the recording companies in America and I recently received an excellent recording—by a blues singer—called "Accentuate The Positive." I played the number over and loved it.

Unfortunately, there are so many recording companies in the States that a lot of first-class numbers get lost in the shuffle.

I'm sure that the sole reason it wasn't a best seller was because it was put out by a small recording company. That way few people got the chance of hearing it. Anyway, I have recorded it myself . . . and, now that it will soon be released on a bigger label, I'm hoping it will get into the charts.

My continual worry — and the worry of most entertainers — is making sure that the public is getting what it wants.

There is always the fear at the back of your mind that one day you may go on stage and find the audience doesn't want you any more.

You finish your act and maybe there will be no applause. If that ever happened to me I'd quit immediately and buy a farm in Virginia.

I began life as a poor boy.

But today I can afford the things I want. I have worked hard for them.

I think, perhaps, some singers find success too easily.

They get to the top on the strength of one recording. This can be a bad thing for them because it doesn't give them the chance to get that essential experience every entertainer must have to ensure lasting popularity.

What I think all show people must work for—whatever particular branch of the business they are in—is perfection.

It is difficult to be a perfectionist without that experience behind you.

My latest recording is "My Heart." It has done quite well—but I must confess I don't like it. I feel I could have done a much better job.

This works both ways. You can cut a disc and think that it's the greatest thing you have ever done. Then you discover everyone hates it.

That's what is so fascinating about this business.

THINGS DO GO WRONG
Eddie, Gene and the UK Tour

FOREWORD
By Bobby Vee

In addition to reading this wonderfully researched story of Eddie Cochran and Gene Vincent's 1960 UK tour I am aware that Spencer has also, subtly and masterfully, managed to reconstruct the English lifestyle setting of the period. Routine comforts and conveniences that we take for granted today were simply unavailable. For travelling minstrels of the day, late night meals were hard to come by. Hotels, built for previous generations, were often old and cold. Travel schedules were difficult and, as this story testifies, sometimes impossible.

One beat at a time, Spencer reminds us that while areas of England were still rebuilding after the devastation of World War II there were sure signs of modernisation everywhere. Like America, Great Britain in the Fifties was enjoying a feeling of good things to come. While the first stretch of the motorway was opening at Preston, Sainsbury's was introducing self service stores. Time was moving on. Overnight, teenagers were gathering at coffee bars and singing about this new rock'n'roll. From the big guitar of Charlie Gracie to Buddy Holly and the Crickets, the Everly Brothers and finally Gene Vincent and Eddie Cochran...the teenage rock'n'roll floodgates had been opened and the show was going on the road. In the midst of it all, Jack Good's interest in the TV production *Six-Five Special* was already shifting to the faster moving *Oh Boy!* As Eddie and Gene toured the UK, their timing couldn't have been better. They were two highly talented but vastly different American rock'n'roll cats. Eddie, with great confidence, had a big dream and a bright future, while Gene was aimless, awkward and self-destructive. They were opposites in the same orbit, who found their way to common ground and friendship and, of course, a heartbreaking story that ends way too soon.

Like well arranged layers of sound, Spencer weaves together statistics, times and dates, radio shows, recording sessions, discographies and details of historic venues (many still productive and many of which I have played myself.). Marty Wilde, Joe Brown and Billy Fury and many others from those ragged and rockin' early days in the UK appear in the book. They were part of the invincible fabric of rock'n'roll...all assuring us that the music wouldn't die. I still believe it's true, and of course, Marty and Joe are still enjoying very successful careers today, while Billy has become a legend.

I'd like to add a couple of personal reminiscences. First, about Eddie. Eddie and I were label mates at Liberty Records and both born in the American wheat belt of the upper midwest. I met him in 1960 at the

Hollywood offices of my producer Snuffy Garrett. Eddie was wearing jeans and a tan shirt and he was very gracious and pleasant. It was a brief but friendly moment in time. The conversation was about music and his upcoming trip to England. I had just recorded my first record for Liberty, a version of Adam Faith's 'What Do You Want', and Snuffy and Eddie were at Gold Star Studio recording 'Three Steps To Heaven' and 'Cut Across Shorty'. They were pumped up about the results. Eddie was backed on the session by Jerry Allison and Sonny Curtis from the Crickets. Sadly, Snuff had just produced what would be Eddie's last session. As performers, if Gene was pure rock'n'roll, Eddie was 'Somethin' Else'...high energy to the walls and over the top: there was a real feeling of let-the-party-begin about him. He was focused, upfront, and a gifted writer, singer and guitar player. The owner of Liberty records, Sy Waronker, loved to tell the story of Eddie's audition which took place in Sy's office in 1957. He talked of "the energy that came out of this little guy belting out song after song." He knew he was destined for big things.

Turning to Gene, between 1957 and 1958 at the Crystal Ballroom in my home town of Fargo, North Dakota and the Moorhead Armory (across the Red River), I saw Gene Vincent and the Blue Caps perform four times in less than a year The first was pure magic unlike anything I had ever seen before, like points of light threatening to burn the ballroom down. The dancers were in a frenzy and it looked like an old Alan Freed movie. Wide eyed girls, hands to faces, were screaming at his every twist and turn, pushing to get closer, and Gene was like a caged animal staring into the spotlight high above the eye line of the audience. He was crouched between two hand-clappers, as if to keep himself from falling or jumping from the stage and destroying himself. All the while, Johnny Meeks was blasting out the staccato guitar notes of 'Lotta Lovin'' until, with an explosion of rim shots, the song ended and the Blue Caps collectively tossed their heads back flipping their caps onto the floor. With that I remember the ballroom owner, Doc Schinn and George the custodian appeared and with watchful eyes, planted themselves firmly on each side of the stage. It was a performance that would never be repeated...at least not at the Crystal Ballroom. Following visits were only met with a variety of diminishing returns but once upon a time I got to really see him...Gene Vincent, the dark and moody Gene Vincent...the leather laden icon of the ragged edged rock'n'roll days.

Things do go wrong, but everything has gone right with this book.

BE BOP A LULA

The STORY of the TOUR 1960

EDDIE COCHRAN

VINCENT

by Bill Morrison
with Spencer Leigh

C'MON EVERYBODY, BE BOP A LULA, WILD CAT, SUMMERTIME BLUES, BLUE JEAN BOP, THREE STEPS TO HEAVEN, SOMETHIN' ELSE, TWENTY FLIGHT ROCK

LIVERPOOL PLAYHOUSE

Mon. JULY 4. – Sat. AUG 13.
Box Office 051-709 8363
Funded by Liverpool, Sefton, Wirral & Knowsley

LIVERPOOL PLAYHOUSE

MONDAY 4 JULY-SATURDAY 13 AUGUST

presents

BE BOP A LULA

By BILL MORRISON
with SPENCER LEIGH

Britain. 1960. On the radio there was Workers Playtime, in No 10 there was Harold MacMillan, but on the streets there was rock 'n' roll. And one show was taking the country by storm.

Gene Vincent and Eddie Cochran were in town and on tour backed by Joe Brown, Billie Fury and Georgie Fame.

But what went on behind the scenes? What happened away from the screaming girls in their bobby sox, and their jealous boyfriends with D.A. haircuts and drape jackets?

BE BOP A LULA tells a story that was not known at the time, of the price two American rock 'n' roll heroes, far from home, had to pay to put on one of the most influential rock 'n' roll shows ever.

With over 50 songs from the period performed live on stage, including Summertime Blues, Three Steps To Heaven, Blue Jean Bop, C'Mon Everybody and of course the title song, BE BOP A LULA has the music, it has the stars, but most of all the story that has never been told.

PAUL CODMAN	BRIAN BENNETT
DAVID EDGE	LARRY PARNES
CHRIS GARDNER	GEORGIE FAME
SHERI CRAMBERT	GIRL WITH SAX
ROB JARVIS	JOE BROWN
GARY MAVERS	BILLY FURY
CATHERINE ROMAN	SHARON SHEELEY
ANDREW SCHOFIELD	GENE VINCENT
MICHAEL STARKE	HAL CARTER
TIM WHITHALL	EDDIE COCHRAN

RADIO AND TV, STAGE SHOWS IN BRITAIN AND FRANCE, A GERMAN TOUR, MORE STAGE SHOWS HERE

They all want Gene Vincent

GENE VINCENT, the American rock 'n' roll singer who guests on three "Boy Meets Girls" shows —on December 12, 19 and 26— and who arrives in this country next Saturday, is going to be one of the busiest stars Jack Good has yet brought over.

He arrives at London airport early Saturday morning to be met by Jack Good, Marty Wilde, The Vernons Girls and representatives from E.M.I. Almost before he has time to get his breath back, he will be whisked across to Broadcasting House for an appearance on "Saturday Club."

The following morning he begins rehearsals for a guest appearance in the Marty Wilde show at the Granada, Tooting. Four days later, on December 10, he is off to Manchester for the first of the "Boy Meets Girls" programmes and also to telerecord for the following two Saturdays.

On December 15 he leaves for Paris where he is booked to do a radio show, and two days after this he is off on a tour of Germany.

Gene Vincent returns to this country on January 6 for a 10-day tour of Granada theatres. And if the response is as good as is expected,

he will probably accept further dates and extend his stay.

And all this started just over three years ago, while Gene was serving with the U.S. Navy, when he composed a tune called "Be Bop A Lula."

Shipmates, liked it, friends liked it and, when he was demobbed, the bosses of one of the radio stations in his home town of Norfolk, Virginia, also liked it—and gave him his own weekly programme.

The next step was a recording contract. So with the odds stacked against him, Gene took "Be Bop A Lula" to Capitol Records. With him went a group which he had formed during his radio days. The Blue Caps.

The result of this audition is history. While the record presses were turning out the first copies of his disc, orders were piling up and Gene Vincent became an overnight hit. "Be Bop A Lula" flew to the top of the charts, and Gene Vincent

and The Blue Caps were booked for personal appearances, tours and television dates.

Then came their first film, "The Girl Can't Help It," which starred Jayne Mansfield. This was followed by an appearance in "Hot Rod Gang."

Meanwhile Capitol were rushing out disc after disc. Among the best known are "Bluejean Bop," "Lotta Lovin'," "Dance To The Bop," "Baby Blue" and "Wear My Ring."

Then came disaster, Gene, who had always been an avid motor cycle fan, had a serious accident. This resulted in his having to wear a leg brace, and even now, it is not absolutely certain that he will ever be completely rid of it.

Recently, in keeping with the trend, Gene and The Blue Caps tried their hand at introducing beaty ballads into their act. This paid off, and so we have such recordings as "Over The Rainbow," "Frankie and Johnny," and even "Summertime" from Gershwin's immortal "Porgy And Bess." Rock may have given way to beat, but Gene Vincent is still as popular as he ever was.   J. H.

EDDIE COCHRAN: WAS THERE EVER A LUCKY BREAK LIKE THIS?

I 'VE heard many stories of artists who have sweated and worked for years for the lucky break that puts them on the road to success. Well, I, too, had a lucky break, although I wasn't exactly looking or waiting for it.

In fact, it was simply a case of being in the right place at the right time!

Let me tell you the story of how I got started. You see, long before I was a singer, I was a guitarist.

I was what is generally known in music circles as a studio musician. That is to say, I played with any number of supporting orchestras on film and disc sessions.

There's no stardom attached to being a studio musician. But I was quite happy and content.

I had plenty of work, and played regularly in the Warner Brothers Twentieth Century-Fox and Capitol studios back home in Hollywood. Then, one day, it happened.

I was sitting quietly in a studio strumming my guitar when up comes a guy and asks: "How would you like to make a picture?"

Well, what would you think? I thought he was kidding, so I played along with the gag and countered with a tongue-in-cheek "Sure!"

Anyway, he tells me he's going to fix it and leaves me saying that he'll phone the next day. I didn't think any more about it. How could I?

I wasn't a singer. I had never made a vocal disc. I had been no nearer a film camera than the adjacent recording studios!

So I was pretty amazed when the fellow DID call the next day. "Can you sing?," he asked. I still thought it was a leg-pull. "You bet," I told him. "Rock 'n' roll?" he queried.

This time I put all my eggs in one basket. "Sure, it's just my style," I replied, chuckling to myself.

His next words really floored me. "I'm sending a new song along to you, and I want you to make a demonstration disc. Let me have it as soon as possible," he said. There was nothing else I could do. Even if I couldn't sing, I had to go through with it.

The song turned out to be an up-tempo rocker titled "Twenty Flight Rock." And I'll make no secret of the fact that after playing it just once, I decided I didn't like it at all.

It's true to say that I was on the verge of throwing in the towel.

But I decided to play ball. I cut a disc with some friends, and, much as I disliked it, I sent the record along to the fellow. Next thing I knew was that I'd been signed for a guest appearance singing the song in the beat film "The Girl Can't Help It."

Well, that's how it all began. The film was my stepping stone to success. Yet even when it was showing in America, I still didn't have a disc contract.

★

Then along came an executive of Liberty Records to get me to sign on the dotted line.

I remember that on my first disc session as a singer, I cut a tune called "Sittin' In The Balcony." Hearing the playbacks after the session was a bitter disappointment. I didn't like the record at all, and felt I could have done so much better.

But I guess all my worrying was for nothing.

The disc—boosted, I suppose, by the release of "The Girl Can't Help It," which let fans get a look at me for the first time—went on to sell a million. I was amazed and I've never really got over it.

Anyway, after that "Twenty Flight Rock" started to sell and so did another little ditty called "Drive In Show." But I've experienced my biggest successes—"Summertime Blues," "C'mon Everybody," Somethin' Else " and "Hallelujah, I Love Her So"—over the last few years.

"The Girl Can't Help It" seems to have had some kind of impact on film producers, because I've since made two films.

One was with Mamie Van Doren in "Untamed Youth" and the other, which still hasn't been screened in Britain, is a guest singing spot in "Johnny Melody."

Apart from some minor parts on TV,

I haven't really tackled any demanding dramatic rôles. But serious acting does interest me, and if the right part comes along, I'll definitely take drama lessons.

But I don't want to do a film unless I really feel I can do justice to the rôle.

Another of my aims for the future is to better myself musically. I still play all the guitar solos on my recordings, but what so many people don't seem to know is that I also play piano, bass and drums. In fact, I've played them all on disc at some time or other.

For instance, by multi-taping techniques, I played guitar, bass and drums on "Summertime Blues" and "C'mon Everybody." I'm pretty proud of these discs because in addition, I also sang the lead vocal parts—including the bass voice on the former—and wrote the songs.

To my way of thinking, "Hallelujah, I Love Her So" is the best record I've made to date, and on this I play piano.

There are also several tracks featuring yours truly at the keyboard on my new album, which is due out here soon.

I guess every young singer around today has been influenced by someone or other, and when people ask me who I look to for inspiration, I have no hesitation in naming the one and only Ray Charles, one of the greatest blues singers of all time.

Have you ever listened to Ray? Perhaps you heard his 1959 hit "What'd I Say?".

Well, if you listened to any of his discs, you'll understand what I mean when I say that he has the most exciting beat sound I've ever heard—or am likely to hear, for that matter.

Ray's music isn't strictly rock 'n' roll. It's more rhythm-and-blues, with spiritual overtones. I don't consciously try to copy him. I simply set out to generate the same exciting feeling that he produces when he sings.

Before I wind up, I must say that my stay in Britain has been one of the really wonderful events in my life.

The fans have been most kind. I've enjoyed playing to them on concert dates, and I only wish I could meet the many millions who watched my "Boy Meets Girls" TV dates.

Anyway, the trip isn't over yet. I'm still having a ball, and I hope my records continue to please you, so that you'll invite me back to this wonderful country again and again.

THINGS DO GO WRONG
Eddie, Gene and the UK Tour
by Spencer Leigh

C'MON EVERYBODY
Introduction

"The formula for Heaven's very simple,
Just follow the rules and you will see,
And as life travels on
And things do go wrong,
Just follow steps one, two and three."
('Three Steps To Heaven', Eddie Cochran)

In 1988 the Liverpool Playhouse commissioned a musical play about Gene Vincent and Eddie Cochran's UK tour of 1960, which was called 'Be Bop A Lula'. My job was to provide the background so that Bill Morrison could write and direct the play itself. He asked one question after another - what were the best and worst theatres? how did they travel? who shared dressing-rooms? did they sign autographs? did they write letters? what happened in-between shows? did anyone have a ritual before the show? who did the washing? was there anywhere to go after a show? how sick was Billy Fury? what was the distance between Sharon Sheeley and Eddie Cochran? Sharon and Gene? Sharon and Billy Fury? The questions never stopped but by talking to the participants, I found the answers. Opinions could be conflicting as the performers and backstage people viewed events from different perspectives.

The play was written around that research and it was as accurate as a two-hour play can be. We deliberately had Joe Brown singing 'A Layabout's Lament' and Billy Fury 'Wondrous Place' even though neither had been recorded at the time. The first showed how views towards unemployment had changed since the early 60s and 'Wondrous Place' was irresistible, a brilliantly atmospheric number for the stage: it amazes me that no contemporary artist has revived this song. We also had Joe Brown backing Gene and Eddie on stage, although he only did this on TV and radio bookings. Minor things really. I remember Joe Brown laughing loudly as soon as the actor playing his manager, Larry Parnes, came on stage. It wasn't a funny moment so why did Joe find it hilarious? "I couldn't believe it," he said, "he's come back to haunt me."

At the time, Larry Parnes was alive but practically out of the business. He had been cooperative and resolved to come from London to Liverpool for the opening. Three days before, I got a call from one of his friends: "Larry's sleeping and I want to ask if there's anything in the play that Larry may feel sensitive about." "If you mean his homosexuality, no," I said, "I wouldn't ask someone to come 200 miles to feel humiliated. However, the musicians do complain about their poor wages." Ten minutes later, Larry rang me. "Thank you for that. I'm looking forward to coming to Liverpool." "You don't mind them discussing their wages?" "Not at all. That's just schoolboys talking about their headmaster behind his back." Larry enjoyed himself that night, even buying the cast and crew a drink. He had one criticism: "When I mention someone who has died, I always add, 'God rest his soul' as a little prayer. Can you please include that?" The next night David Edge as Larry Parnes said, "Eddie Cochran, God rest his soul." At the time, Gene was sitting on Eddie's coffin and Larry was persuading him to continue touring.

'Be Bop A Lula' played for 13 weeks in two runs at the Liverpool Playhouse and had two national tours. The reviews were generally terrific, although Jack Tinker's bad-mouthing in the 'Daily Mail' dashed its West End hopes. Tinker felt it was a history lesson and loathed the scene in which Eddie showed Joe Brown some guitar techniques. To me, it was worth the ticket price just to see the spotlight on Andrew Schofield's black-gloved hand as it reached through the curtain and took the microphone as he launched into 'Be Bop A Lula'. Tim Whitnall and then Martin Glyn Murray of the Mock Turtles made excellent Eddie Cochrans. Unfortunately, out in LA, Eddie's girlfriend Sharon Sheeley heard poor reports about the play and we never hit it off. I sent her a photograph of the pretty actress (Catherine Roman) playing her but she said, "That's nothing like my nose." Sometimes you just can't win but she wanted to get her own film about Eddie off the ground and maybe we were jeopardising that project.

Unlike most rock'n'roll bio-plays, 'Be Bop A Lula' did not take the audience through a performer's life. It simply covered the UK tour and ended shortly after Eddie's death. The play ended with Gene, back on the road, singing an anguished 'Be Bop A Lula' and it's clear that Gene has died mentally.

Plays about backstage life are commonplace but 'Be Bop A Lula' seemed to work on several levels. It was about British rock'n'rollers meeting their American heroes: it was about two strangers in a strange land: it was about two Americans who seemed much older than their British counterparts: it was about coping with fame, and, most of all, it was about the early days of rock'n'roll - the pioneering spirit, if you like. One critic thought we had written a gay play as it was about the friendship between Eddie and Gene.

Bear in mind that Eddie and Gene were very different - sure, they both liked rock'n'roll and they both liked to drink, but Eddie was self-assured while Gene was lacking in confidence. Gene had peaked but Eddie felt he had a lot to offer.

Because of the length of my interviews and because I was being encouraged to answer unusual questions by Bill Morrison, I amassed an unexpected amount of detail about the tour. After the play, I filed the material away and got on with other things. When I wrote 'Wondrous Face', a biography of Billy Fury, for Finbarr International in 2005, I revisited my files for research and realised what a wealth of material I had accumulated. I feel it is my public duty to have it published.

I would like to counter one possible criticism. With a misguided sense of loyalty, Gene Vincent's fans often rush to his defence when his wayward lifestyle is criticised. I'm sure they feel that such criticism distracts from the quality of his music. Far from it: I love Gene Vincent's unruliness and it enhances the music for me. I don't think anybody would want Gene Vincent for a next-door neighbour but he's a great character to write about as there was always tension when he was around. Gene and Eddie were real, three-dimensional characters and are not in any way manufactured pop stars.

Spencer Leigh
October 2007

Acknowledgments

Thanks to all the interviewees and to 'Hit Parade', 'New Musical Express' and 'Melody Maker' for permission to copy articles from contemporary publications. We cannot trace the copyright owners for 'Disc' and 'Record Mirror, but we acknowledge their contributions. I wish to thank all my interviewees and also Steve Aynsley (editor of the Gene Vincent fanzine, 'Git It!'), the late Bob Azurdia (who interviewed Larry Parnes at length in 1988), Bill Beard (editor of the fanzine, 'The Eddie Cochran Connection'), Johnny Black (backonthetracks.com), Billy Butler, Trevor Cajiao (editor of 'Now Dig This'), Stuart Colman, Peter Darke, Geoffrey Davis, Derek Glenister, Richard Havers (and his dad!), Derek Henderson, Nick Jones, Mark Lewisohn, Mick O'Toole, Graham Spittles and Ian Wallis (author of the superbly researched, 'American Rock'n'Roll: The UK Tours, 1956-72'). The superb news cuttings on www.eddie-cochran.info saved me hours of research in reference libraries and, as well as being the most tireless investigator and authority on all things Vincent, Derek Henderson maintains a brilliantly informative website, www.spentbrothers.com. There is also significant background material in the BBC Written Archives in Caversham. If only, the ITV companies had maintained similar archives. Above all, I would like to thank John Firminger for his illustrations and James Cullinan at Finbarr International for his faith in this book. James is always the first reader and he only commissions books when he knows he wants to read the story himself.

Hank and Eddie,
The Cochran Brothers

EDDIE COCHRAN....Liberty 55070...................................ONE KISS

MEAN WHEN I'M MAD.................(Simon-Jackson, BMI)
(Simon-Jackson, BMI)
Cochran follows his "Sittin' in the Balcony" hit with another strong
one. "One Kiss" is an appealing moderate-beat tune with rockin'
chorus backing and teen-bait lyrics. Flip is also an effective rock
and roller, but "One Kiss" has edge, performance-wise. Both sides
should pull plenty of play.

SITTIN' IN THE BALCONY

JOHNNY DEE

EDDIE COCHRAN
on Liberty Records

EDDIE COCHRAN
(Liberty 55144)

B "SUMMERTIME BLUES" (1:53)
[American BMI—Cochran, Cape-
hart] Strong gimmick combo-vocal
support is the big attraction in this
Cochran sung opus about a fella trying to quit summer work so he can
pay more attention to his gal. A deep-
voiced artist portrays his boss, congressman, and father. Humorous r&r
ditty.

B "LOVE AGAIN" (2:11) [Amer-
ican BMI—Sheely] Cochran effectively plays the disillusioned lover
in a good-sounding soft-beat roman-
cer.

EDDIE IN THE MOVIES

Best Wishes

from
EDDIE COCHRAN
Currently Featured in 20th Century-Fox
"THE GIRL CAN'T HELP IT"
Personal Management
JERRY CAPEHART   GENERAL *Representation* ARTISTS CORPORATION

EDDIE COCHRAN
Summertime Blues; Love Again
(London HLU8702)★★★★

EDDIE COCHRAN can usually be relied upon to produce an ear-catching noise, and he lives up to his reputation with **Summertime Blues.**

To hand-clapping and rhythm he goes off on a tricky beat excursion with **Summertime Blues.** Deep male voice supplies some interjections in between Eddie's choruses on this side. Very good production attempting to get something different out of current styles.

Love Again also produces some variations on the beat—and I think it will help the disc to be very commercial. A slow ballad here with some good gimmicks that I think you'll find pretty arresting.

Given some airings I'd say this was one that could easily hit the parade.

Eddie looks set to click with 'C'mon'

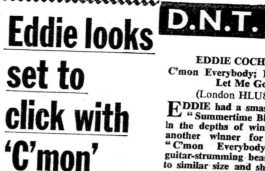

D.N.T.

EDDIE COCHRAN
C'mon Everybody; Don't Ever Let Me Go
(London HLU8792)

EDDIE had a smash with his " Summertime Blues." Now in the depths of winter he has another winner for us. His " C'mon Everybody " is a guitar-strumming beat song cut to similar size and shape as his previous big one. Compulsive stuff which has the right noise to make it a consecutive click for Cochran.

Don't Ever Let Me Go." with slight change of tempo also uses echoing effects as Eddie chants this beater.

Contrasting side which will have its devotees. Eddie certainly has the measure of the market at the moment.

FARMILIAR RING

EDDIE COCHRAN
Teenage Heaven; I Remember
(London HLU8880)★★

TEENAGE HEAVEN is a strutting rock number which has Eddie laying down the law about the kind of house he wants. If you think the melody sounds familiar, you will not be wrong. It is "Home On The Range " with a brand new set of lyrics !

It does not strike me as being so potent as Cochran's previous successes.

Nor does I Remember, a slow beat number which Eddie handles well enough. Lyric may set a few hearts fluttering, however.

1. NICE GUY EDDIE
Eddie Cochran at home

"I want a house with a pool, shorter hours in school,
And a room with my own private phone."
('Teenage Heaven', Eddie Cochran)

In 'Boll Weevil Song', Eddie Cochran refers to Oklahoma City as his home town, but in truth, he had rarely been there. He told reporters that he came from Oklahoma City as his manager advised him that it sounded better than a small town.

His father, Frank Cochran worked as a factory machinist in Oklahoma City and he and his wife, Alice, had their first child, Gloria, in 1924. Frank worked through the Depression but money was hard to come by, especially with a large family to feed – there was also Bill, Bob and Patty.

In 1938, the family moved to Albert Lea, Minnesota, a town with 15,000 inhabitants, some 100 miles south of Minneapolis. It was a farming community, growing corn and soya beans and breeding pigs, but Eddie's father worked at a packing company and later was a garage mechanic. On 3 October 1938, their fifth child, Edward Ray Cochran, was born. It was the same day that Neville Chamberlain told the House of Commons that he had secured "peace in our time".

While they were living in Albert Lea, Eddie was shot in the right leg during a hunting expedition with his brother, Bob. He was in bed for several months and unlike Gene Vincent, he followed medical advice. His leg recovered almost completely – more about this later.

When he was 12, Eddie wanted to join the school orchestra. He considered drums, trombone and clarinet before settling on guitar, although there was no opening in the orchestra for a guitarist. His parents bought him a guitar and his brother Bob showed him some chords. He had heard country and western because of his parents' tastes and now he played along with the radio, listening to stations from Chicago and Detroit and acquiring tastes for jazz and R&B.

After doing his military service, the eldest son, Bill settled in Los Angeles with his wife, and the Cochrans joined them in 1951. Bill found them a house in Bell Gardens, one of the poorer suburbs of the city. Eddie didn't know anyone when he moved to California and he called the guitar his best friend.

Eddie enrolled in Bell Gardens Junior High and he befriended Fred Conrad Smith, known as Connie and later Guybo. He played double-bass in the school orchestra and could also play steel guitar and mandolin. By late 1953, they were in a trio and they would rehearse in Bert Keither's music store. They would play anywhere locally, usually for the experience.

Despite having relatively small hands, Cochran became a proficient guitarist.

In October 1954, Eddie met a country singer, Hank Cochran, who was three years older and also lived in Bell Gardens. He was a professional musician and he asked Eddie to join him. Though unrelated, they did resemble each other and they began performing in fairs and dances as the Cochran Brothers. They hosted their own radio show, 'California Hayride', in Los Angeles.

In 1955, the Cochran Brothers supported Elvis Presley on a show in Dallas and overnight, Eddie wanted to play rock'n'roll. They rushed to Memphis to audition for Sam Phillips at Sun Records but he wasn't interested. The trip was still worthwhile as they did some recordings for another Memphis label, Ekko. The first single was 'Mr. Fiddle' and 'Two Blue Singin' Stars', a tribute to Jimmie Rodgers and Hank Williams. They played the 'Town Hall Party' in Compton, Los Angeles each week, a televised live country show, and also appeared on the 'Big D Jamboree' in Dallas.

At the Bell Gardens Music Centre in October 1955, Eddie met a 28-year-old songwriter, Jerry Capehart. He had been in Korea and had fronted a Japanese country band. He thought of being a lawyer but he worked as a part-time musician and wanted to write hit songs. He hired the Cochrans to record some demos and they backed him on his single, 'Rollin''. He secured a contract for them with a Hollywood publishing company, American Music. They had the freedom of their demo studios and the possibility of releasing records on the company's Crest label.

In April 1956 Eddie recorded 'Pink Pegged Slacks' for American Music. It was derivative of Carl Perkins' 'Blue Suede Shoes' and it marked Cochran's first recorded attempt at rockabilly. The Cochran Brothers also sang rock'n'roll on their Ekko single, 'Tired And Sleepy'/'Fool's Paradise'. They toured Hawaii as the opening act for country star, Lefty Frizzell.

In July 1956, Eddie wrote an answer version to 'Long Tall Sally', 'Skinny Jim', which gave a nod to Gene Vincent with its line, "Be bop a lula, Skinny Jim." This, his first solo single, was released on Crest but did nothing. Eddie accompanied Wynn Stewart ('Keeper Of The Key', a song popular enough for Presley, Perkins and Lewis to jam on the Million Dollar Quartet) and veteran country star Skeets McDonald ('You Oughta See Grandma Rock'), which is regarded as a rockabilly classic.

On some demos at Goldstar Studio, Eddie, through overdubbing, played all the guitar parts with Jerry sometimes using a cardboard box, with suitable tape echo, for percussion. You can hear the cardboard box on 'Blue Suede Shoes'. The recordings demonstrate how Eddie was learning studio techniques, but they are not always effective. 'That's My Desire' sounds like a Neil Innes parody, with Cochran's voice distorted, a night-club piano and Capehart's box-slapping.

Jerry Capehart played Cochran's work to Al Bennett, a co-founder of the relatively new Liberty Records. Eddie was given a contract with Liberty but he continued to make demos at American Music. In a short but complicated career, he worked as a session musician and recorded for such American Music subsidiaries as Silver Capehart, Crest and Zephyr. The records were by the Kelly Four (which was Cochran's regular backing group), Jewel and Eddie, Lynn Marshall, Darla Daret and others. 'Guybo' was an instrumental with Eddie on guitar.

With its strong links to the film industry, Liberty Records was asked to supply artists for a satire on rock'n'roll, 'The Girl Can't Help It'. As soon as the producer Boris Petroff saw Eddie Cochran, he realised how photogenic he was. He gave Eddie a demo of 'Twenty Flight Rock', which was written by Ned Fairchild, and asked him to learn it. Cochran could hardly believe his good luck and he recorded the song in Goldstar with Connie Smith on bass and Jerry Capehart thumping his cardboard box. The countdown in the tongue-twisting lyric is a nod to 'Rock Around The Clock' and the performance itself can be seen as a pastiche of Elvis Presley's Sun records, although it works as a *bona fide* rock'n'roll performance. The urgency of its rhythm complements the idea of someone running to the top of an apartment block. As often happened, the composer had to share his songwriting credit with the performer.

Eddie was excited about appearing in 'The Girl Can't Help It' and rather than being intimidated by the rock'n'roll celebrities in the movie, he thought it could be his big break. Eddie twitched his way through the breathless 'Twenty Flight Rock', a very tricky song to mime. Eddie shuffled and shrugged his shoulders in a sensational screen début even though he is miming and on screen for less than two minutes. Playing a gangster, Edmund O'Brien hilariously comments on his actions. 'Twenty Flight Rock' was not a UK hit but when John Lennon met Paul McCartney at a fête in Liverpool in July 1957, they discussed its lyrics and, indeed, the song was the glue which bound them together. The film had played at the Forum Cinema on Lime Street in Liverpool for seven weeks, perhaps indicating how desperate Liverpool teenagers were to hear rock'n'roll: there was little on TV. As a neat coincidence, John's mother, Julia, had worked as an usherette in the Forum during the 1930s.

Cochran was immediately given a role in a second film, 'Untamed Youth' (1957), in which he sang 'Cotton Picker and supplied another, 'Oo Ba La Baby', for 'the girl built like a platinum powerhouse', Mamie Van Doren, Van Doren was a poor man's Jayne Mansfield, who in turn was a poor man's Marilyn Monroe.

As luck would have it, his single at the time of 'The Girl Can't Help It' was the smoochy, gulping rockaballad 'Sittin' In The Balcony', which Eddie recorded with the Johnny Mann Singers. The song was written by

John D Loudermilk and it became Eddie's first Top 40 single, making No.18 in May 1957. Although Cochran appreciated its potential, he never cared for it. Still, the girls were now screaming at concerts. He met Gene Vincent for the first time on a package show in Philadelphia. He appeared on several TV shows, notably Dick Clark's 'American Bandstand', and in June 1957 at the Opera House in Chicago, he stole the show from headliner Tab Hunter: admittedly, not a difficult task.

The follow-up single, 'One Kiss', was a cynical rewrite of 'Sittin' In The Balcony' and the single missed the Hot 100. A further attempt was made with 'Drive-In Show', which, with its ukulele had a 1930s feel, and that reached No. 82. Eddie was teased about this record as "I bet my peanuts to a candy bar" sounded suspiciously like "I bet my penis to a candy bar" and he would later tell his friends that he was the first to put a penis on record. Although only having one hit single, Eddie was allowed to cut an album, 'Singin' To My Baby', the only one to be released during his lifetime.

Eddie was in demand as a session musician and he was involved with many singles for unknown artists who remained unknown. For example, Ray Stanley was no vocalist but his singles feature some stunning guitar sounds from Eddie Cochran. Eddie played guitar and sang backing vocals on the seasonal novelty by the Holly Twins, 'I Want Elvis For Christmas'. Eddie enjoyed it all, not least because it was extra income.

Just to show how times have changed, what singer today would dare sing, "They call you cradle baby, But you're just right for me", yet when 'Billboard' reviewed Eddie's 1957 single, they wrote, "She may be young, but she's just right for him."

In January 1957, Bill Haley and his Comets made the first tour of Australia by rock'n'roll stars. The second package was in October 1957 and featured Little Richard, Gene Vincent, Eddie Cochran, Alis Lesley ('the female Elvis Presley' or so they claimed) and local star, Johnny O'Keefe. The poster attributes the songs 'Butterfly', 'Gone' and 'A White Sports Coat' to Eddie Cochran, which means that they had him confused with Charlie Gracie, Ferlin Husky and Marty Robbins. The tour was booked for 31 shows but it was cut short when its star performer, Little Richard found religion. Like Gene, Eddie couldn't understand why Little Richard had to quit the tour. Nevertheless, 25 shows were completed in 12 days, and they also undertook radio and TV commercials. Cochran acquitted himself well. The fans took to him and he made a show of mopping his brow with a handkerchief and throwing it out to the audience.

Jack Davey's Ampol Show was broadcast in Australia on 11 October 1957 and included Eddie Cochran performing 'Whole Lotta Shakin' Goin' On' with his customary huskiness and showing that when he covered a song, he didn't simply ape the original. The insidious arrangement included Eddie referring to himself in the lyric: there are indications that, like Jerry Lee Lewis, this would have become a trademark. Jack Davey gives him a travelling rug for his trouble so he won't be cold when he tours.

Cochran returned to the US for another package tour, 'The Biggest Show Of Stars For '57', which featured Chuck Berry, Fats Domino, the Everly Brothers and Buddy Holly with the Crickets. Phil Everly introduced him to his date, 17-year-old Sharon Sheeley at the Paramount Theatre in New York City. They would not meet again for some months but Sharon was struck (and stuck) on Eddie from the start.

Jerry Allison of the Crickets recalls, "Eddie held a party in New York City and the cops came and broke it up. He said to one of the cops, 'You wouldn't do this if I was Eddie Cochran.' 'No, I wouldn't,' said the cop. 'Well, get out then', said Eddie Cochran."

Eddie Cochran started 1958 intent on making rock'n'roll records. His 'Twenty Flight Rock', released way too late in November 1957, hadn't been a hit. Now he was rocking with a vengeance, but 'Jeannie Jeannie Jeannie', a wild rocker with a frantic guitar break, only made the charts for one week at No.94. His voice was gruffer than before and well suited to the song, which, strangely enough, was loved by his mother. 'Pretty Girl', the next single, was more of the same.

The TV heart-throb, Ricky Nelson, topped the US charts with 'Poor Little Fool', which was written by Sharon Sheeley. She passed another song 'Love Again' to Jerry Capehart, who told her that Eddie would cut it. When she went to the studio, she wasn't sure whether he would remember her but they became good friends.

In March 1958, Eddie helped out on the LP, 'A Gene Vincent Record Date'. The sessions were between 25 and 29 March with Eddie arranging and playing bass. He can be heard on 'The Wayward Wind' and his deep voice introduces 'Git It', a glorious mix of doo-wop and rock'n'roll which precedes the Beach Boys. On 28 March he had a day off and while Gene recorded George Gershwin's 'Summertime', Eddie cut 'Summertime Blues'. Jerry Capehart had challenged him with the words, "There has never been a blues about summer." Everything goes wrong for the teenager in the song and the lyric offered no solution: "There ain't no cure for the Summertime Blues." The frustration was accentuated with strummed chords and yet his performance had the humour of the Coasters. Cochran played lead guitar and rhythm, Connie Smith was on bass and Earl Palmer on drums. Jerry Capehart and Sharon Sheeley were handclapping. And like Gene Vincent, Eddie knew how to use a 'Well'. In April 1958, Eddie and Gene headlined the Youth Rally at the Chicago Stadium and did further dates together.

Guitar ace and former Hellecaster, John Jorgenson, comments: "I don't know to this day how Eddie Cochran got that sound on 'Summertime

Blues', which is a really cool record. It sounds like a guitar that was played at half-speed; it sounds like an acoustic guitar up an octave, but I don't know. Eddie Cochran used acoustic guitar for some great percussive sounds. The combination of the way he and Buddy Holly used it and of course Elvis Presley on the early Sun sessions set the tone for most bands in the 60s with rhythm and lead guitars. A lot of 50s bands didn't have drums and that could create the illusion of drums being there. Eddie Cochran made use of the six-string bass as well, that real twangy sound at the beginning of 'C'mon Everybody' is a Danelectro six-string bass. It was not replacing the bass but it was doing a low, twangy six-string bass part, which was great."

Lyricist Tim Rice: "Eddie Cochran is one of my great heroes, not just for his music but also for his lyrics. The lyrics of 'Summertime Blues' and several others are just so direct and so intense and so right on the button. In under two minutes, 'Summertime Blues' has a go at almost everything that annoyed young people in 1958 – it has a go at parents, school, work and then the Government. And it does it brilliantly with lyrics that would easily stand up in a Broadway show: 'I called my congressman and he said, quote, "I'd like to help you, son, but you're too young to vote."' That is superb and it tells you about the dishonesty of politicians and the pathetic attempts by ordinary citizens to get through."

In September 1958 'Summertime Blues' made No.8 on the US charts, the only time Eddie Cochran made the US Top 10. You'd have thought that 'C'mon Everybody' couldn't have been a better follow-up, but it only made No.35 in the US. Eddie called rock'n'roll music 'bubblegum': he enjoyed doing it but he knew it wasn't suitable for night clubs.

Wally Whyton of the UK skiffle group, the Vipers: "When 'Summertime Blues' was coming out, the publishers said to me, 'It's your type of song: do you want to cover it?' We went electric for the occasion. I bought a pick-up, plugged it in and though we tried hard, we couldn't get what Eddie Cochran had. You've got to do the Elvis thing on a song like that and we were just anglicising it."

In December 1958, Eddie and Sharon went to New York where he was appearing in a package show at Loew's State Theatre for the DJ and impresario, Alan Freed. Freed asked him to appear in the film, 'Go, Johnny, Go', which featured Chuck Berry, Ritchie Valens, Jackie Wilson and the Cadillacs. The way he dances with his guitar is most entertaining, and it summed up Eddie Cochran. He loved his guitar and always had it with him. 'Teenage Heaven' was his first production by Snuff Garrett, who filled out the sound, but the single only scraped into the Hot 100. Eddie was generally obliging but for some unknown reason, he declined an appearance on 'The Ed Sullivan Show'. He performed in the Sands Hotel, Las Vegas, very much against his better judgment.

Eddie appeared on package shows with Buddy Holly and the Everly

Brothers. He was set to appear on the 'Winter Dance Party' with Buddy, Ritchie Valens and the Big Bopper but he dropped out after a mix-up over bookings. Just as well as the tour was not designed for the artists' comforts and the weather was appalling. Buddy, Ritchie and the Big Bopper were killed in a plane crash on 3 February 1959. Within days of their deaths, Eddie recorded the narration, 'Three Stars', with the intention of passing the royalties to their families. It could have been among the first charity singles but Liberty had no facilities for organising this. The song became a US hit for Tommy Dee and a UK one for Ruby Wright. After Cochran's death, his manager, Norm Riley would tell journalists that Cochran had missed the flight with Buddy Holly, but this was nonsense.

Buddy Holly's death played upon Eddie Cochran's mind and he did not want to die in an air disaster. He cut down on touring and only played clubs around his home. He concentrated on studio work. He thought that instrumentals were going to be the next big thing and he cut several including the dynamic 'Eddie's Blues'.

New technology was coming to the record industry. An innovator in electric guitars and multi-track techniques, Les Paul had recorded 'Mockin' Bird Hill' and 'How High The Moon' with his wife, Mary Ford way back in 1951 and the world was catching up. Cochran was impressed. He also loved the work of the country guitarist, Chet Atkins.

With some candour, Eddie told an interviewer that the biggest drawback of being well known was that he didn't have the time to associate with his friends: "You see, back home I like to hang around with a gang of old friends, but the publicity men don't like this. They get mad at me and say I go out with the wrong people. I like the company of my old buddies, so it's very confusing." His sister, Gloria, said, "He lived at home – he always did. He'd be gone for weeks at a time and there would be times I wouldn't see him for a while, but he was really happy when he was home – he loved his home."

Eddie was an all-American boy and when he was home he went on hunting or fishing trips. He had a passion for firearms and loved demonstrating his quick draw. A fellow musician and friend, Gene Ridgio, said, "Eddie always carried a Buntline .45 revolver which had a 13 inch barrel as well as a .22 calibre quick draw six-gun – all western style. We would go up into the mountains and Eddie would shoot things off."

Gene Vincent biographer, Rob Finnis: "One reason why Eddie and Gene were so close was because they shared a love of guns. Gene was very envious of Eddie's Buntline Special. Eddie, of course, collected guns as a hobby, but Gene liked them in a stupid, malicious way. Gene used to go round to Johnny Cash's house a bit and practice his quick-draw in front of Johnny's mirror. When Gene was in Germany in 1962, some idiotic fan gave him a loaded Luger and he brought it to England. He used to wave it around a lot and his wife had him up for using it in September '63."

When Sharon Sheeley was writing another song of teenage anguish, 'Somethin' Else', she asked Eddie's brother Bob for details of various US cars and they went into the lyric. She gave Bob a songwriting credit and Eddie recorded the fiery song. The single made No.58 in the summer of 1959. Another song, 'Weekend' was recorded with the Kelly Four, but would not be released until after Eddie's death. Indeed, what is surprising is the number of tracks that Eddie had in the can.

Eddie nurtured a love of Ray Charles and in October 1959, he recorded 'Hallelujah I Love Her So' for a single, playing both rhythm guitar and piano. Liberty thought highly of the recording and they added strings prior to release, although Eddie preferred it without.

Unquestionably, Eddie had the image to be a great star, possibly a film star. As good-looking as Presley, he had blue eyes, honey-coloured hair and weighed ten stone. He said, "If I'd known about moving like he does, I might be in Elvis's shoes right now." Eddie had developed some great stage movements of his own where he shrugged his shoulders and also moved his guitar in a circular motion, rather like the pistons of a locomotive. Eddie had special 'breakaway' suits manufactured, which meant that after a mauling by his fans, his clothes could be stitched back together again in 15 minutes. Eddie played a red Gretsch 6120, sold to him by Bert Keither. It was a Chet Atkins model, which had little volume on stage from its normal pick-up. He replaced the pick-up with a Gibson Humbucker, a unit that had clarity, depth and volume. He added a Bigsby tremelo arm, which enabled him to devise rich two-chord endings for some songs.

In October 1959, Eddie Cochran turned 21: he had had plenty of experience and he was well set to become a major star. He had the looks, the vocal ability, the guitar technique and he knew how to arrange and produce records. The problem was how he wanted to do it. There is an interview with Brian Matthew for 'Saturday Club' when he is in the UK. When Brian asks him about his ambitions, Eddie says, "I want to be successful." That is the key to Eddie Cochran. He had the versatility to do whatever the public wanted and if romantic beat-ballads were going to be the rage in 1961, then, heck, he would do them too. In a Q&A for 'Hit Parade', he said that his aim was to be "as successful as Sammy Davis Jr". This is a totally different attitude to Gene Vincent whose philosophy, if he ever thought about it, would be "Let's do the time-warp again."

Bobby Vee: "I enjoyed the rough edges of rock'n'roll and you can hear the dark side in Eddie Cochran and Ronnie Hawkins. They made records that made parents say, 'This music is never going to last but it's going to corrupt our youth.' By the time I got involved, the songs were socially acceptable and spoke of values that are still alive today."

The 'New Musical Express' printed a first person article by Eddie

Cochran (clearly ghosted as it gets a few facts about his life wrong), in October 1959, but he states that his fondest wish is to come to the UK. Tours tend to be set up well in advance – they have to be – and so it looks as though Eddie already knew he was coming over in January 1960 and this was a good way of putting his name forward.

One of Eddie Cochran's last performances in the US was in the Moonlite Gardens, Wichita, Kansas in November 1959. A reporter, Bill Fergusson, listed Eddie's repertoire: 'C'mon Everybody', 'Kansas City', 'Twenty Flight Rock', 'Sittin' In The Balcony', 'Milkcow Blues', 'Hallelujah I Love Her So', 'Three Steps To Heaven', 'Somethin' Else', 'Drive-In Show', 'What Am I Living For ' (a tribute to the late Chuck Willis), 'Don't Ever Let Me Go' 'Cut Across Shorty', 'Boll Weevil Song' and 'Summertime Blues'. Unfortunately, Eddie never performed a set as long as this in the UK and usually performed seven or eight songs.

At the turn of the new decade, things were going well for Eddie Cochran but he was about to race with the devil.

Gene and The Bluecaps
In the Girl Can't Help It

Tommy Facenda,
Gene and Paul Peek
in 'Hot Rod Gang'

Crazy Beat; (right) Gene
onstage in Japan with Jerry
Merritt (right) and (below)
Japanese rock'n'roll combo

Rock'n'Roll at the Capitol
Tower, Gene in the studio

GENE VINCENT ROCKS!

COVER PERSONALITY

GENE VINCENT

DISC cover spot this week is devoted to an artiste very much underrated — Gene Vincent. Our mailbag consistently shows what a strong following he maintains with Britain's pop fraternity.

Why he should have been missing from the popularity charts is one of those interminable puzzles of the record business that it is always impossible to answer.

Gene has turned out many exciting records, all having the qualities that the public seemed to demand yet, apart from near-hits, he has never really rung the bell continuously in this country.

His debut on wax in Britain, at a time when worse recordings were reaping rewards, made a considerable impact but the promised interest has not been sustained.

We first heard of this vibrant singer through his distinctive treatment on "Be-Bop-A-Lulu," a fast - moving composition which was coupled with an unusual echo chamber effect.

The repeated echo was enough to bring this record to the attention of many, for it was certainly novel and stimulating.

It sold in vast quantities and, in the States, the disc reaped a good harvest for the Capitol organisation.

The search which the company had made to find a rival to Presley then looked like paying off with big dividends.

Twenty-year-old Gene was the successful competitor from the 200 would-be record singers auditioned by Capitol.

As soon as he could be whipped into the studios he was cutting his first disc, "Be-Bop-A-Lula" coupled with "Woman Love."

From the beginning it appeared that Gene Vincent was destined to be a formidable entrant on the rock field. Many more disc issues followed, each one improving with experience, yet the real hit target seemed to elude him.

Gene Vincent was born in Norfolk, Virginia, and, like many youngsters, Gene found that he was able to put his youthful voice to good use in church choirs.

Additionally, he was constantly surrounded by country and folk music and, not unnaturally, he acquired an interest in this class of singing.

HE STILL WAITS FOR A UK HIT

A visit to Virginia in his early teens was to make a considerable impression on Gene Vincent. He heard, for the first time, a group of negroes singing their kind of music and, such was the effect on him he started transposing all his pop song favourites into their style.

But he was also to realise that his efforts were but an imitation and that he wasn't singing in his own true style. Gradually he developed his own presentation—one which he felt, and knew, was just right.

Meanwhile, though money was scarce, he saved hard and long so that he might possess a guitar. Once it was bought, Gene then had to teach himself to play it.

His guitar was also soon to make him a popular shipmate for, at the age of 17, Gene Vincent joined the U.S. Navy.

Throughout his service days he not only amused himself in his off-duty moments, but he was a regular favourite with the ship's company whenever they had musical evenings.

On his release from the navy, Gene returned to his home town in Norfolk, where he soon fixed himself up with a radio series on the local station.

His fame, apart from a few local concerts, went little farther and it was not until the record audition presented itself that Gene suddenly found himself quickly propelled up the star ladder.

Apart from the string of excellent waxings to his credit on singles, Gene Vincent has three dynamite - packed LPs

which have become big favourites with his followers. They are "Bluejean Bop," "Gene Vincent Rocks and the Blue Caps Roll," and "Gene Vincent and the Blue Caps." The Blue Caps, of course, are a strong feature on all the Gene Vincent waxings.

Friday (August 15) Gene Vincent has a new disc issued— "Yes I Love You Baby" coupled with "Rocky Road Blues." It is another excellent recording by the young American singing star who so much deserves that elusive big hit.

Seen here with the Blue Caps, Gene Vincent has another try this week for that elusive hit.

Doug Geddes

2. DON'T FORGET THAT I'M A WILD CAT
Gene Vincent at home (if there was such a thing)

"I guess I was just born lucky."
(Gene Vincent, December 1959)

Up to the 1960s, there are two types of stars. Elvis Presley, Frank Sinatra and Marilyn Monroe are in the first category, artists who keep their distance from their audiences, and may even be worshipped like gods. Then there are the friendly, boy-next-door types and examples from the rock'n'roll world are Buddy Holly, Pat Boone and the Everly Brothers. Meet them on the street and they exchange friendly greetings. It's not that one category is *ipso facto* more talented than the other: it's just the way they present themselves. Rock music has thrown up a third category: performers you would do your best to avoid, performers who are dangerous, either to the public or to themselves and maybe to both. Kurt Cobain, Sid Vicious, Marvin Gaye, Janis Joplin and even John Lennon at times are examples, and the role model is Gene Vincent. Admittedly, both Jerry Lee and Chuck Berry have displayed similar tendencies but not consistently and not in the way that Gene Vincent did. An example from the film world of the 50s would be Robert Mitchum and Gene certainly had something of Mitchum about him.

Gene Vincent toured incessantly - it was all he knew once the hits stopped coming - but even though he met many people, very few can say they really knew him. He instilled fear, and with his heavy drinking, the self-destruct button was pressed. The physical reminders of his motorcycle accident could always be seen, but were the mental scars just as severe? Did he suffer from what is now recognised as post-traumatic stress disorder or was he just a highly unpleasant psychopath? Did his detractors make enough allowances for the pain he suffered and the fact that he had endured two major accidents?

The old jazz song, 'Sailing Down The Chesapeake Bay', sounds romantic but there was a lot of poverty around Norfolk, Virginia. Still, it promised a better life for the Craddocks and the Coopers, two families from North Carolina. They had moved independently to Norfolk, Virginia. Ezekiah Jackson Craddock, known as Kie, married Mary Louise Cooper, known as Louise, in 1934. Their son, Vincent Euguene Craddock, was born on 11 February 1935 and was always known as Gene. His sister, Evelyn was born in 1938. The family was poorly educated and could be described as white hillbillies.

In 1942, the family moved to Munden Point near the North Carolina border, and Kie opened a general store. When Gene was seven, he sang 'Little Sir Echo' in a school show, a prophetic choice as his records were to be bathed in echo. He loved the country and western music that he heard on the radio. Because there was a considerable black population in Munden Point, he experienced blues and gospel at first hand. According to Evelyn, "We'd leave the house and sneak over to the black church and look through the window. They did a lot of hand-clapping; they were very active with their hands, and hallelujahs."

Gene was never forthcoming about his childhood or indeed anything, but the child was the father to the man. In addition to those musical influences, he watched western and war films. He had a collection of toy soldiers and even then, yearned to own guns and knives. He loved fairgrounds, especially the roller-coasters. His lack of education made him suspicious: he needed help in signing contracts but those who were helping him may have been bleeding him dry.

Although his family was poor, he kept bugging them for a guitar and then, when he had one, for lessons, but he never had the application to go far. He would often spend his afternoons on the porch of the general store, singing with anyone who passed by. Two more sisters followed – Tina (born 1948) and Donna (born 1949) – and then the family returned to Norfolk. The city was a naval base and Kie worked in the shipyard. As Gene was not as big as others of his age, he was bullied, but bullies would regret it as he had a vicious temper and was tougher than most. Gene was disappointed at being too small for his school football team. Possibly to compensate, Kie signed the papers to allow him to join the navy on 19 February 1952. He had just turned 17 and he wanted to experience action in Korea.

At first he was a deckhand and then a boiler-man. In January 1954 his ship, the Chuckawan, began a four-month tour of the Mediterranean and when he returned, he was given the National Defence Service Medal and the Navy Occupation Service Medal (Europe), although he had done nothing particularly courageous. He still loved music and he bought a guitar in Italy for $22 and would sing quietly and wistfully to himself: his favourite song, 'Red Sails In The Sunset', had a naval connection. He may not have had a girl in every port but he had a succession of girlfriends and when he was home, he rode a small, cheap motorcycle.

When his three years' service was up, he re-enlisted for a further six. For this, he received a cash bonus and he replaced his motorbike with a powerful Triumph. He fancied being in a club of racing hooligans like Marlon Brando in the biker film, 'The Wild One'. He loved black R&B and the new music that was coming up, which merged country with R&B and was called rock'n'roll.

In July 1955, Gene rode his Triumph to visit a girlfriend. In Franklin, a small town close to Norfolk, a woman in a Chrysler ran a red light, smashing into Gene's bike and crushing his left leg. The police claimed the accident was Gene's fault and it was settled out of court, largely because Gene had signed papers while under heavy medication. He was not awarded any compensation but he did receive medical pay from the navy of $136 a month, which Gene said kept him in cigarettes. For the rest of his life, Gene was incensed about the way he had been treated and, indeed, he had grounds for complaint.

The doctors wanted to amputate Gene's leg but when his mother visited him, he made her promise not to sign the papers as he was under 21. Unfortunately, Gene was so keen to get back into action that he ignored medical advice, and as a result, he remained in constant pain for the rest of his life. The problem was a wound about the size of a £2 coin just above his ankle. He had several operations but he felt that the doctors had got it wrong and he would talk to anyone and everyone about suing them for $1m.

One consolation was that he began writing songs in hospital. 'Be Bop A Lula' was inspired by the comic strip, 'Little Lulu' and he co-wrote it with another patient, Donald Graves. He wrote 'Race With The Devil', which reflected his attitude to life. He was once in a T-Bird, which was passed by a Buick. He said to the driver, "Hit it, man! Let's blow them off the road!" They raced up to 120 mph and Gene was mad when the driver refused to continue. Whether that's true or not, I don't know: Gene might have heard 'Maybellene' and simply decided to write another song about a car race.

Despite his injuries, Gene began dating 15-year-old Ruth Ann Hand and they were soon engaged. His mother said, "Gene's romances were always in a whirlwind. He went steady with her for three months and although he was engaged several times, this time he did marry." The marriage took place on his twenty-first birthday, 11 February 1956, and Gene wore his naval uniform. As Louise was against the marriage, they lived with Ruth Ann's parents.

February 1956 was a momentous month for Gene as on the 5th, he watched Elvis Presley perform at the Monticello Auditorium in Norfolk, Virginia. The radio station WCMS held talent contests and although Gene was shy, he won with his version of Elvis's current hit, 'Heartbreak Hotel'. This led to bookings on the WCMS radio show, 'Country Showtime', and a Chevrolet dealer allowed Gene the use of a Chevvy in return for singing at his car lot every weekend.

One of the radio DJs, Sheriff Tex Davis, whose title was as phony as Colonel Parker's, saw Gene as a means of making money, but, to be fair, he had recognised his talent. In April 1956, he sent a tape to an A&R man at Capitol Records, Ken Nelson, who was searching for his own Presley. Ken Nelson invited Gene and some local musicians to Nashville, Tennessee. They went to Owen Bradley's studio. Nelson had assembled some session musicians but when he saw that the so-called Blue Caps were competent, he let them go. Following the new rock'n'roll sounds, Bradley had devised an echo chamber and to ape the success of 'Heartbreak Hotel', it was used to its full extent on 'Be Bop A Lula'. Not one to miss a trick, Sheriff Tex bought a further piece of the action by securing Donald Graves' share of 'Be Bop A Lula' for $25.

There is no doubt that the recording débuts of several rock'n'roll stars are extraordinary: many of the elements that constitute Fats Domino's sound can be heard on 'The Fat Man' (1949); Elvis Presley's 'That's All Right (Mama)' (1954) is a very confident, exciting performance by a 19-year-old; Bo Diddley began with his signature song, 'Bo Diddley' in 1955, the same year that Chuck Berry told us about 'Maybellene'. But did anyone beat Gene Vincent's 'Be Bop A Lula'?

'Be Bop A Lula' begins with Gene's protracted 'Wel-l-l-l-l-l-l', which became his vinyl signature as surely as a painter signs his pictures. In two minutes, we have the essential Gene Vincent. All his vocal characteristics are here: his strange pronunciation, his breathless delivery, his high-pitched dexterity and above all, a tremendous presence which gives the record a neurotic edge. The record is so intense as he is desperate to tell you about this girl with an implausible name. It was a remarkable achievement for someone on his first record date.

'Be Bop A Lula' was no one-off performance that day. He also recorded its B-side, the utterly bizarre 'Woman Love'. This heavy breathing rocker was banned by the BBC for being too suggestive. "Let's face it," said a spokesman, contradicting himself, "it's suggestive and you can't understand what he's saying anyway." Presumably the BBC misheard "I'm lookin' for a woman with a one-track mind, A-huggin' and a-kissin' and a-smoochin' all the time", or was Gene saying "a-fuggin'" or worse all the time.

That first session reveals that the Blue Caps was a top-class backing unit, although their flat blue caps were better suited to greyhound racing. No one bothered with their individual names in 1956 but Cliff Gallup is amongst the greatest rock'n'roll guitarists. Cliff's chance to shine came with the third track they recorded that day, 'Race With The Devil'. It sounds frenzied now, so imagine what it sounded like in 1956. As Gene's drummer, Dickie Harrell, wore a blue cap, the group was named the Blue Caps and Gene, to his credit, insisted that they were billed on the record label.

Gene's family thought 'Be Bop A Lula' was terrible but they were used to country music. Capitol's promotion called him 'The Screaming End' and described 'Be Bop A Lula' as a 'novelty record'. Gene received national exposure on 'The Perry Como Show' and the single climbed to No.7 on the national chart.

Bad leg or not, a rock'n'roll star's popularity depended on his availability: he could not be married. Ruth Ann was told that if she went on the road, she would be passed off as Gene's cousin. Soon Gene was having one night stands – he told one fan magazine that his hobby was 'taking young girls to the movies' - and Ruth Ann tired of his flirtations. Gene returned to his parents and she filed for divorce. She received $1,000 and a Cadillac. As

Gene Vincent and his Blue Caps could command $1,500 a night, it wasn't generous. Despite, or perhaps because of, his handicap, Gene slept with an enormous amount of women. To quote one Blue Cap, "Gene couldn't tell you on a Tuesday whom he'd slept with on the Sunday."

Gene was already an erratic performer. At one gig, he punched his fist through a wall and refused to go on stage. He often broke his cast on stage. He liked to duet 'Hound Dog' with other singers with them pointing fingers at each other and going, "You ain't nothin' but a hound dog."

When Gene was booked to appear at the Sands Hotel in Las Vegas, he hated it because there were no teenagers in the audience. He started drinking heavily while he was there. A piece of sheep's bone that had been grafted onto his leg was broken and the month-long booking was cut short so that he could have treatment at the Veterans Hospital in Portsmouth. Tex Davis, who had soon fallen out with Gene, excused his shortcomings by saying, "The boy was always in pain. He had to see a doctor in every town."

And he saw little of the money. The British TV producer, Johnny Hamp, who produced his Granada special in 1964 says, "Gene Vincent told me that 'Be Bop A Lula' had sold 3 million copies the first time round and yet he had made no money from it. His manager told him that you just made records for publicity purposes."

Tax returns show that Gene Vincent and his Blue Caps earned $330,000 in 1956, but the line-up changed as musicians tired of his behaviour. He appeared in the film, 'The Girl Can't Help It', with Jayne Mansfield, Eddie Cochran and Little Richard, and he kept the band together by telling them they'd see 'Jayne Mansfield's jugs' if they stuck with him. I doubt that they did as they only made a quick cameo appearance, but Jayne was told to chat up Elvis Presley to see if he would join the guest list. As he didn't, we can only assume that he didn't see Jayne Mansfield's jugs either. Gene's new guitarist, Paul Peek, gives a 'real gone' performance in 'The Girl Can't Help It' and all but steals the scene. Gene's leg was still in plaster and so the director covered his open toes and painted a shoe on the cast, although in the end, his feet aren't shown on the screen. Gene started wearing a leg-iron in June 1957.

Gene was always spending money. He bought a Cadillac Coupe de Ville and he would buy new shirts rather than wash them. He asked his drummer, Dickie Harrell to look after his clothes and Dickie would find tens and twenties in the pockets. He would leave $20 tips for waitresses and the band would go back and reclaim them. Gene used to joke that Dickie bummed money for hamburgers and saved his own money, later coming to Gene in a Cadillac and saying, "Thanks, Gene." Gene's behaviour was scarcely normal. He fired the Blue Caps a hundred times over and once when he lost a card game, he threw a bottle of whisky through a TV screen.

At the end of 1956 Cliff Gallup, Wee Willie Williams, who had just got married, and Jack Neal left the Blue Caps and Cliff Gallup was so disillusioned that he took a regular factory job. Ken Nelson told Gene to contact Ed McLemore, a promoter in Dallas, who ran the live radio show, 'The Big D Jamboree'. For a year from May 1957, Gene, his girlfriend, at times his parents and his band were to live in a ranch-style house in Dallas. He developed a new band with Johnny Meeks, but Dickie had had enough and quit. They toured in a 1957 Ford wagon and trashed motel rooms. Gene was featured in another film, 'Hot Rod Gang', and how about this for irony? In May 1957, Johnny Cash, Gene Vincent and Jerry Lee Lewis played five shows as a benefit for the police department in Beaumont, Texas.

Although they had only been together for a day, Gene Vincent had befriended Eddie Cochran on the set of 'The Girl Can't Help It'. In September 1957 they went to Australia for a tour with Little Richard. Little Richard felt the Russian Sputnik satellites were a sign from God that all was not right with the world and as a declaration of his new-found faith, he threw his expensive rings off Sydney Harbour Bridge and renounced rock-'n'roll. Gene said that he wanted to dive in after them and without its star, the tour was soon abandoned.

Australian music writer, Jon Stratton: "Australia in the 50s was even behind England. Television didn't start here until 1956 and then it was only in Sydney and Melbourne. It came in because of the Olympic Games in Melbourne, and it was introduced to the other capital cities in 1959. Restaurants, other than silver service places, were hard to find until the late 70s, although there were some Greek and Italian restaurants because of the immigration of Greeks and Italians after the war. There was no inner city development until Kings Cross in Sydney in the mid-60s. The tour by the Beatles was a huge shock to Australia. There were massive crowds, certainly as big as anywhere else. Because of Australia's 'White Australia' policy, most Australians had never seen a Negro. Louis Armstrong came to Australia before Little Richard but there were very few."

Since Ruth Ann, Gene had had several girlfriends, notably a Canadian singer Monique and a New York girl Jacqueline. In Klamath Falls, Oregon, Gene met a divorcée, Darlene Hicks, who was working in the box office for the show. He dedicated 'Wear My Ring' to her and held her hand on stage. He mimed on 'The Ed Sullivan Show' where he was denied a microphone stand, his main prop. He phoned Darlene and asked her to join him for Christmas. He married her on 1 May 1958: she was 19 and her daughter, Debbie, two. Her father was a truck driver and both parents were devoted to the Assembly of God.

By the standards of rock'n'roll performers, Gene Vincent recorded prolifically for Capitol, making several albums as well as singles. He had a flexible voice and could handle both wild rockers and tender ballads with ease – his 1957 B-side, 'Important Words', is exquisite. However, he never built upon the success of 'Be Bop A Lula'. The follow-up, 'Race With The Devil', mysteriously stopped at No.96 and then 'Bluejean Bop', 'Crazy Legs' and 'Five Days, Five Days' found no takers at all. Gene didn't return to the Top 100 until a year later with 'Lotta Lovin'', an infectious rocker with the novel introduction of two clapper boys, at No.13 and following 'Dance To The Bop' (No.23), that was it. The tortuous 'Baby Blue', the up-tempo version of Bill Monroe's bluegrass song, 'Rocky Road Blues' and Johnny Meeks' stunning rocker, 'Say Mama' did nothing at all. Reading over this paragraph, I can hardly believe what I have written. I suspect that the quality of the records was irrelevant and other factors were at work.

For a start, Gene had alienated himself from many American DJs. He would fail to turn up for interviews and, if he did, he might be inarticulate and mumbling. When Gene played a DJ convention for Dick Clark, he was asked to sign his cheque over to him. He said over the microphone, "You're all assholes like Dick Clark and you can go and get fucked." Again I doubt the veracity of this story, but Gene was fond of telling it.

Capitol Records was a legitimate organisation which refused to have anything to do with payola (plays for cash), hence they had few hit records. Also, Elvis Presley had gone in the army, Little Richard had found religion, and Chuck Berry a prison cell. Rock'n'roll was turning saccharine: artists like Bobby Rydell, Frankie Avalon and Fabian were clean-cut, good looking and no trouble. Gene Vincent was thuggish, drunk and vulgar.

Paul McCartney gives a good indication of what Gene was like on the road: "I got to know Gene in Hamburg when he was at the Star-Club. He was the star and we were the supporting group. Gene had been a marine and he was forever offering to knock me out. Marines can do that sort of thing: they touch your two pressure points. I'd say, 'Sod off', but he'd say, 'Go on, Paul, you'll only be out for a minute.' I always resisted that. I didn't fancy being unconscious, thank you very much."

1958 was a disastrous year for Gene Vincent and his Blue Caps. One of them crashed a car, a couple were arrested for being with under-age girls, and another was beaten up by a Mountie. Gene was arrested for wrecking a motel room, being drunk around minors, and performing a lewd show. His management had to agree to indemnify hotels so that he and the Blue Caps could stay there, and remember that this is years before the Who and the Sex Pistols.

Gene owed $60,000 to the Revenue and when he didn't pay, they took possession of the house in Dallas. He didn't believe in lawyers so he didn't contest the assessment: typical Gene Vincent behaviour – he accepted what-ever happened to him but he always complained. Gene and Darlene moved in with friends of hers. It would prove to be a stormy relationship but that applies to all Gene's relationships – a subsequent wife was nicknamed 'Rocky' because of her constant black eyes. In Darlene's case, she hated him drinking and he hated her talking to old acquaintances. She once called the police and asked them to control him. He was always supremely jealous and his blues song from 1959, 'Darlene', is surprisingly revealing:

"Darlene, Darlene,
How comes you treat your daddy so mean,
Darlene, Darlene,
How comes you treat your daddy so mean,
Well, you're so lazy, woman,
You never keep your daddy's clothes clean."

Gene got so fed up on one tour with the Blue Caps that he left them without pay and facing a $500 hotel bill. The Blue Caps reported him to the Musicians' Union and he lost his card. But that's the way he was: Gene was always arguing with someone – managers, wives, friends, musicians. He never got along with anyone for long. He wasn't a person you could joke with as he might turn on you.

When I met Ian Dury, the writer and performer of 'Sweet Gene Vincent', during a West End run, he had a photo of Gene on his dressing-room wall. "I wasn't bothered about being crippled myself so I didn't relate to Gene Vincent because of that - no way. Look at that picture I've put up of him in that car. That's when he was happening and had nice clothes, and that's before Jack Good got hold of him. There's two years of his career that I like. After he got a saxophone in, I didn't like him anymore. I like the voice and the vibe that he had for a couple of years in the 50s when he had a good band. Songs like 'Woman Love' and 'Race With The Devil' are the pure Gene Vincent songs. They are really fantastic. I wouldn't have gone to see him after 1958 but I saw a BBC2 documentary about him and that was extremely tragic."

In 1959, in a much scaled-down operation, Gene drove to gigs on his own and rehearsed, if you can call it that, with local musicians. He would get lonely and feel sorry for himself, particularly if he was holed up in Alaska. Darlene, wanting to cheer him up and how's this for love, joined him in Alaska. She gave birth to their daughter, Melody Jean, on 27 April 1959. His record producer, Ken Nelson got fed up with taking calls from Gene asking for money.

Gene began working with the strong-willed guitarist Jerry Merritt: he got on with him "because he wouldn't take the crap like some other guys," says Darlene, "He had a strong personality and just shrugged it off." Jerry recalled Gene swallowing two bottles of Aspirin a day and washing them down with beer and whisky as well as endlessly smoking. Gene took Jerry with him for five dates in huge auditoriums in Japan. He rang Darlene every day and would argue with her. He walked out of the tour and the promoter told Jerry to impersonate Gene and finish the dates. None of the Japanese audiences complained.

Gene Vincent had never recaptured the glory of 'Be Bop A Lula' in 1956, but his career lacked any purpose or shape. The contrast with Eddie Cochran is marked as Eddie was very mindful of his career: not everything worked out for Eddie but he knew how to build on his experience. Gene, on the other hand, was a jobbing rock'n'roller and any success came to him by accident. His failures were partly his own doing – he was tetchy, awkward and utterly disorganised – but it is possible to sympathise with him as he lived in constant pain. His face became haggard and drawn and he lived in a show-biz environment where good looks were highly prized. By the end of 1959, he was 24 years old and his American career was all but over. If they made a film of his life, the strapline might be "A chip on his shoulder, a brace on his leg…"

ROCK BRITANNIA

BACK IN THE USA

ANGLO - AMERICAN

Queens of Song

Left; Ruth Brown, right; Lita Roza

MR. BLUE SUEDE SHOES IN PERSON
CARL PERKINS
Hear Him Rock·n·Roll

JOHNNY CASH
"CRY CRY CRY" *Get Rhythm*
THE TENNESSEE TWO

WARREN SMITH
Rock & Roll Ruby

"OOBY DOOBY" ROY ORBISON

EDDIE BOND
Rockin Daddy

THEY Rock and Roll
DON'T MISS
THE ALL STAR SHOW

FRIDAY, JUNE 1
3:00 P.M.
Advance Tickets
Adult $1.00
Children 50c

BOB NEAL RECORD SHOP
(Higher at the door)
OVERTON PARK
SHELL

GREAT SONGS - GREAT ARRANGEMENTS
SHAKE, RATTLE AND ROLL
Recorded by DEEP RIVER BOYS (H.M.V.) and
BILL HAYLEY AND HIS COMETS (Brunswick)

JUST SOME OF THE STARS IN
6·5 SPECIAL
ANGLO AMALGAMATED FILM DISTRIBUTORS LTD.

listen to
Record Round-up
EVERY SATURDAY NIGHT 11.30 to 12.30
RADIO LUXEMBOURG
208 metres
JACK JACKSON
introduces hits on ~
DECCA-GROUP RECORDS

Voted the Top Rhythm and Blues
Favourite of 1954 in the States
Honey Love
Records by: Dennis Lotis with Ted Heath (Decca)
Bunny Paul (Columbia)   Vicki Young (Capitol)
ORCHESTRATIONS IN THE PRESS

CHARLES L. TUCKER presents

ROCK 'N' ROLL
—UP TO SEE

The Queen's Jester

MAX WALL
★ ANNE HART ★
at the Piano FRANK PORTER

THE FIVE SPEEDACS ☆ THE JUMPIN' JAX ☆ THE SIX TEEN-AGERS

SEE MAX WALL ROCK 'N' ROLL WITH
TERRY KENNEDY
and his ROCK 'N' ROLLERS

£50 IN CASH PRIZES
GREAT ROCK 'N' ROLL COMPETITION !
1st PRIZE £25 : 2nd PRIZE £15 : 3rd PRIZE 10.
HEATS EVERY PERFORMANCE MON.- FRI.. Semi-
Finals 1st House Sat. :   Finals 2nd House Sat.

Tour Opens HIPPODROME, BRIGHTON, MARCH 18, 195

Picked by The Cash Box
and Billboard—and
they're so right! Like
Money In The Bank!
MONEY HONEY
CLYDE McPHATTER
AND
THE DRIFTERS
1006

Above;
Max cashes in

Advert far Left
The Real Deal

40

3. LOVING THE ALIEN
Britain and the US in the late 1950s

"England and America are two countries separated by a common language."
(George Bernard Shaw)

In 1998, Paul McCartney's terraced home under the blue suburban skies of a Liverpool estate was restored and opened to the public. Most visitors view this ole house as a Beatles' home but it also provides a unique view into family life of the Fifties. The house was built by Liverpool Corporation for £1,370 in 1952 and it is painted in their favoured maroon and cream. Unlike many of the high-rise developments, the house feels like a home, but there are few of today's comforts and time-saving devices. There is no fridge-freezer, no microwave, no double-glazing and no central heating. The downstairs toilet is outside, which would be decidedly unpleasant on a cold and rainy night. There is a small Pye television bought for the Coronation in 1953, a primitive twin-tub washing machine and a 1950s electric cooker. The living room carpet is made from turkey runners - four strips of stair carpet stitched together. There are three types of wallpaper in the living room, a common practice of the time. Paul's mother was a midwife, so the family had a telephone, one of the few on the estate of 330 houses.

Because fresh food could not be kept for any length of time, it was necessary to go shopping daily. The corner shops provided a personal service and many were suspicious when Sainsbury's introduced self-service stores in the late Fifties. Few ate out - coffee bars were introduced for teenagers, thereby suggesting that full meals were out of the question. Cafés served English food, and when Dean Martin sang of 'a big pizza pie' in 'That's Amore', few people knew what he meant. Gene Vincent wanted a pizza after a Sunday show in Cardiff in the 1960s. It might have been possible in London, but in Wales late on a Sunday night, absolutely no chance.

In 1958 we saw the start of jet travel and the first stretch of motorway was opened at Preston. The country, like the world, was getting smaller. The Canadian professor, Marshall McLuhan, used the phrase, 'the global village', to refer to electronic communication bringing everyone closer, but it applied to transport as well.

In the 1950s, the merchant seamen working on the cruise liners from Liverpool to New York, mostly as cooks and waiters, became known as Cunard Yanks. As one of them says in the documentary film, 'Liverpool's Cunard Yanks' (2007), "Liverpool was black and white but when we went over to New York, it was Technicolor." They returned with the latest fashions and music. Modelling themselves on the film star Tony Curtis, they looked cooler than anybody else and would stand out in the city's dance halls.

The film tells the story of six of them, who brought back to Liverpool as much of America as they could afford. One explains that although he only earned £23 a month, the tips from wealthy passengers could take it to £200. An American jukebox was purchased for a Liverpool pub, and the new owner was delighted to find it stacked with US singles. Ivan Hayward bought a Gretsch guitar in Manny's Music Shop in New York for $310. It captivated a young George Harrison who gave him £70 for it (with an IOU for another £20). How Ivan and his pals got their purchases through Customs isn't explained, but usually, crew members were allowed through without hassle.

This film skilfully contrasts the difference between the US and UK culture in the 1950s and demonstrates that we were envious of our American cousins and thought that America represented the high ideals of living. We had fallen behind because of six intense years of warfare and a poor resolution to the aftermath. The Second World War ended in 1945 and many UK cities had been devastated. In retrospect, the politicians made inexplicable decisions, rebuilding German cities before reshaping their own. For many years, the remains of bomb damage could be seen in British cities and even now there are remnants.

In 1961, Robert A. Heinlein wrote 'Stranger In A Strange Land', a science fiction novel about a Martian who comes to Earth and grapples with its culture. Heinlein didn't need a Martian for his theories: he could have written about Eddie and Gene coming to the UK. The two all-American lads were unprepared for the culture shock that awaited them. Of course, it would have been nothing like touring the USSR, if such a thing were even possible, but it was because they expected the cultures to be similar that the differences became so marked. Both Eddie and Gene liked late-night TV: there was nothing in the UK and indeed, not even TVs in their hotel rooms. In 1950, the BBC held a monopoly with just one television channel, but only 40,000 sets had been sold. The coronation of Queen Elizabeth II in 1953 was an enormous boost for sales, so much so that a second channel, ITV, which was reliant on advertising, began broadcasting in 1955. Within a few years, ITV had topped the ratings with 'Sunday Night At The London Palladium' (hosted by Tommy Trinder and then Bruce Forsyth). The top-rated BBC TV variety show was 'The Billy Cotton Band Show'.

Both these programmes were very theatrical, but the whole nature of theatre shows has changed today. By and large, the main act will do 90 minutes and there will be an opening act, usually an acoustic singer-songwriter or a club comedian. In the 1950s, it was different. A star act like Vic Oliver or Tommy Trinder might only be on stage for 30 minutes and the rest of the show would be singers and specialist acts like ventriloquists, animal trainers, memory men, strongmen, trick cyclists and dancers. In 1957, the highly strung balladeer, Dorothy Squires refused to participate in a variety tour rather than accept second billing to a new American rock'n'roller, Charlie Gracie. When rock'n'roll became popular, it became clear that teenagers were bored while waiting for the star act – Buddy Holly's tour of 1958 is a good example - and so rock'n'roll package shows were devised. In particular, the UK impresario and manager, Larry Parnes, took his lead from Alan Freed's package tours in the US.

Britain wasn't always allowed to copy America. In the early days of ITV, the contributing companies wanted to ape the US quiz shows. They wanted a '$64,000 Question' but weren't permitted to give away that amount of money, and nor did they have it to give away. The ITV equivalent was called '64,000 Question'. The public wondered, 64,000 what? 64,000 sixpences was the answer, that is, £1,600!

British TV quiz shows were cosy and comfortable. ITV's top game shows, 'Double Your Money' with Hughie Green and 'Take Your Pick' with Michael Miles, both came from Radio Luxembourg. In 'Take Your Pick', you could win five shillings if you could go a minute without saying 'Yes' or 'No'. Quite a difficult task and I hope the lucky participants didn't spend their winnings all at once.

The BBC's top panel game was 'What's My Line?' with Eamonn Andrews and featuring David Nixon, Lady Isobel Barnett, Barbara Kelly and arch-grump, Gilbert Harding. Robin Day, by the way, was already being criticised for his rude, aggressive questioning on news programmes. Jackie Rae and Marion Ryan presented 'Spot The Tune', while Jeremy Hawk presided over 'Criss-Cross Quiz', a TV version of noughts and crosses. Someone I knew took part in one of the first editions: no one in the production team had appreciated that the game could end in a draw, and he and his opponent had the first one.

Unlike America, there was no daytime TV to speak of and if Gene and Eddie had switched on in the hotel lounge, they might have caught schools broadcasts or 'Andy Pandy' and 'The Flowerpot Men'. How would a programme like 'Listen With Mother' fare today: 'Listen With Motherfucker' would be more like it.

Vance Packard's acclaimed book on American advertising, "The Hidden Persuaders' (1957), pointed out the dangers of media manipulation, but the persuading was hardly hidden. If an advertisement was on TV, it was abundantly clear that someone wanted to sell you something. Advertising slogans became national catchphrases including "Go to work on an egg" (devised by Fay Weldon), "Drinka pinta milka day", "You can't tell Stork from butter", and two famous straplines for newspapers – "All human life is there" ('News of the World') and "Top people take 'The Times'".

They weren't 'movies' then, they were 'films'. And you didn't go and see one film - you got a double-bill, usually with the news, trailers and local adverts as well. The public often went to the cinema to see the news, and there were queues the week after the Grand National, no matter what the main feature was.

A new technique, Method Acting, was expounded by Lee Strasberg at the Actors Studio in New York. The character had to be built up from within and the psychological aspects of the role were emphasised in order to heighten realism. Method Acting called for improvisation and some actors of the older school, including Frank Sinatra, resented the new kids on the block. Much to his chagrin, Sinatra had to co-star with Marlon Brando in 'Guys And Dolls' (1955) and couldn't understand why 'Mumbles' was allowed to sing. Another Method actor, James Dean, had a meteoric rise and a tragic end, crashing his Porsche on the way to a race.

A similar realism entered musicals via Leonard Bernstein and Stephen Sondheim's 'West Side Story' with its aggressive choreography and songs for delinquent gangs in New York, although admittedly no gang of toughs would really be dancing like that in the city streets.

The western was still very popular during the Fifties and several directors extended the genre by making films that were more than gunfights. American Indians were still the bad guys and an otherwise great film like John Ford's 'The Searchers' (1956) would therefore be politically incorrect today.

The UK showed itself to be more tolerant than both the US and South Africa, which followed policies that shame them now. In 1956 Ted Heath and his Orchestra appeared with Nat 'King' Cole in Birmingham, Alabama. There were two houses, one for whites and one for blacks, and segregation was so strict that even the performers on stage had to be kept apart. The Ku Klux Klan had decided to kidnap Nat 'King' Cole whilst he was singing. Fortunately, the plot was unsuccessful and six men were arrested, but during the fracas in which Nat twisted his foot, Ted Heath instructed his orchestra to do the decent British thing and play 'God Save The Queen'.

Nearly every adult smoked, and clubs and pubs would now be seen as health hazards. In 1954 the link between smoking and lung cancer was established, but it made little difference to cigarette consumption during the Fifties. The manufacturers put up a smokescreen and the Platters were right: 'Smoke Gets In Your Eyes'. The Brits yearned for American or French cigarettes: they particularly liked the flip-top packaging of American cigarettes. You could extract them so coolly from the packet. Similarly, American chewing-gum looked so much more inviting: the long thin strips of Wrigley's wrapped in silver paper as opposed to hard, white tablets.

It was a time of sexual repression. Despite all the casual liaisons during the War, the accepted standard was that you did not have sex unless you were married. Getting someone in the family way was frowned upon: unless there were medical reasons, abortions were illegal, and the song, 'I Could Have Danced All Night' was effectively 'I Should Have Danced All Night'.

The contraceptive pill was developed during the Fifties and this came into its own in the Swinging Sixties, and, indeed, was one reason it was called the Swinging Sixties. The relationship between men and women changed radically as females discovered a much greater independence.

Teenage music was in short supply on both radio and TV, but the BBC's first pop programme, 'Six Five Special', started in 1957. Its producer, Jack Good, moved to ITV for the faster-moving 'Oh Boy!' Some TV variety shows were imported from America, notably 'The Perry Como Show', but as there were no Ed Sullivan or Steve Allen broadcasts, we were denied Elvis Presley's controversial appearances. The vigilant Musicians' Union had banned miming and US shows like Dick Clark's 'American Bandstand' were also not broadcast.

The British alternative to rock'n'roll was skiffle, cheaply played on acoustic guitars, washboards and string-bass. Hundreds of skiffle groups were formed, but the King of Skiffle, Lonnie Donegan, was far more polished than his acolytes. The craze was short-lived, largely because Donegan himself wanted to progress. It also had no American appeal to speak of: American teenagers had more money and could go straight to electric instruments like the Beach Boys or, indeed, Eddie Cochran.

British rock'n'roll stars had more charm than menace. Tommy Steele with his million watt smile couldn't compete with Elvis Presley's sullenness, but he chose engaging material like the early Lionel Bart composition, 'A Handful Of Songs'. Cliff Richard started on ITV's 'Oh Boy!' as an untamed rock'n'roller but he switched to gentle ballads like 'Living Doll' (Lionel Bart again) and 'Travellin' Light'.

In the early, pre-Beatle Sixties, the fashion was to have smartly suited, good-looking, flat-stomached youngsters like Eden Kane, Adam Faith, Danny Williams and Jimmy Justice singing beat ballads and wanting to be all-round entertainers. They smiled a lot and behaved impeccably – no swearing, no fighting, no controversial views and no lewd mannerisms on stage. Their managers treated them like puppets. What goes round comes around as the *Pop Idol* winners are precisely the same. They are chosen by pop managers and groomed as family entertainers and nothing illustrates this more than the number one CD, 'Pop Idol – The Big Band Album'. Why are these youngsters working as lounge singers? Gareth Gates was swinging 'Mack The Knife' and Darius Danesh crooning 'Let There Be Love'. Their arena tour closed with Will Young singing 'My Way': the one thing they surely weren't doing was doing it their way.

Surprisingly and quite by coincidence, nearly all the progenitors of rock-'n'roll ran aground in the late Fifties:

October 1957 - Little Richard announced his retirement and joined the ministry.

March 1958 - Elvis Presley joined the US army and hardly recorded for two years. Elvis surmised, "I don't think rock and roll will die out before I get back but if it does, I'll sing ballads." Exactly the way Eddie Cochran would have viewed it.

May 1958 - Jerry Lee Lewis entered the UK with his 13-year-old wife and second cousin, Myra, and was hounded out a few days later.

October 1958 - Carl Perkins' brother and rhythm guitarist, Jay, died of cancer, causing Carl to drink heavily and lose interest in show business.

February 1959 - Buddy Holly, Ritchie Valens and the Big Bopper were killed in a 'plane crash with a pilot unqualified for hazardous conditions.

July 1959 - After a rock'n'rollin' start, Bobby Darin turned sophisticate with 'Mack The Knife'.

November 1959 - The American DJ and instigator of rock'n'roll, Alan Freed, was accused of accepting bribes for playing records.

December 1959 - Chuck Berry was arrested for corrupting a minor and received a two year prison sentence.

Maybe it was a good time for Gene and Eddie to come to the UK.

Break-of-dawn greeting for 'The Screaming End'—

GENE VINCENT

WHEN Gene Vincent arrives at London Airport tomorrow (Saturday), there will certainly be no shortcomings in the welcoming party. In spite of the fact that he is due to arrive at 6.55 a.m., there will be coach loads of fans who have got out of bed at the crack of dawn to greet him.

Jack Good and a few of the Vernons Girls hope to be there—not forgetting EMI executives and the Press. Gene's first few hours in Britain will be rather hectic—after the welcome-in reception, he will appear in BBC's " Saturday Club," which goes on the air exactly three hours and five minutes after his plane touches down !

The following day, he rehearses with a group led by Firing Squad member and singer Joe Brown for his guest appearance in "The Marty Wilde Show" at Tooting Granada the same day. After that he may find some time to relax before he travels to Manchester on Thursday to rehearse his "Boy Meets Girls" spots.

Three shows

Apart from his British TV debut a week tomorrow, he will telerecord two other performances for screening on December 19 and 26.

Unlike many visiting Americans, Gene may find it difficult to select songs for his TV appearances. Recent visitor Jerry Keller was riding high with "Here Comes Summer" at the time he was over here; the same applies to The Browns, whose version of "The Three Bells" has only just started to drop from the Charts.

Gene, however, cannot claim a hit for about three years. In spite of that, every record he has made has become a firm favourite with his

By IFOR GRIFFITHS

British fans and he commands a loyal followi..g.

Many of his discs have come very close to an actual Chart placing and, next to Frank Sinatra, he is one for the Capitol label's best-sellers.

To get in at the start of Virginia-born Gene's career, we have -to go back to 1956. Shortly after Elvis Presley created a sensation in America with his wild singing style, along came an 18-year-old lad with an even wilder style—so outrageously loud, he was immediately dubbed " The Screaming End."

Yes, Gene Vincent had arrived ! He stormed the Charts on both sides of the Atlantic with his very first disc—" Be-Bop-A-Lula."

Gene's follow-up, " Race With The Devil," was a second success—both here and in America. Towards the end of 1956, he scored his third major hit with " Bluejean Bop." Unfortunately, this proved to be his last big success, although all subsequent singles, two EPs and five albums have sold well.

His powerful rocking style has a pronounced country - and - western flavour to it, no doubt due to Gene's interest in folk music during his youth. When he was a mere 12-year-old, he used to delight in listening to the Negro folk songs he heard on visits to a Virginia backwoods store.

He managed to borrow a guitar from a friend and that began " The

Screaming End." During his spell in the U.S. Navy, where he served most of his time in Atlantic tankers, he entertained his naval friends who considered his style a little crazy. But after demob he was urged to audition for Station WCMS in Norfolk, Virginia.

Against his better judgment, he swallowed his nervousness and put in a bid for a part in a show called " Country Showtime." After the try-out, he went home and waited, frightened he had been overlooked, and even more scared when he heard an announcement to the effect that he had been selected for the show !

But he need not have worried. The series was a terrific success—mainly due to Gene's residency. Capitol Records got to hear of the young Mr. Vincent and soon had him signed to a contract.

Latest disc

His summer release on this label "Right Now"/"The Night Is So Lonely" stimulated quite a bit of interest over here and to coincide with his visit, Capitol issue "Wild Cat"/"Right Here On Earth" today (Friday).

Gene's considerable versatility is well displayed on his most recent LP, " Sounds Like Gene Vincent," on which he switches from out-and-out rock to a tender and moving version of the straight ballad, "Now Is The Hour."

British fans have so far been unable to see Gene in the flesh, although he has appeared in two films screened in this country, "The Girl Can't Help It" and "Fury Unleashed," which was seen here early this year.

After his initial visit, Gene will fly to Paris on December 15 for a radio show and then on to Germany, but he will be back on January 6 for a 12-day concert tour of the Granada circuit.

Incidentally, Gene owns a farm in California for when he retires from singing—but I'm sure that won't be for a very long time !

GENE VINCENT GIVEN A GREAT WELCOME

HUNDREDS of rock 'n' roll fans gave American singing star, Gene Vincent, a terrific reception when he made a guest appearance in the Marty Wilde Show at the Granada, Tooting, on Sunday.

Later, in his dressing room, Gene said: "That was some welcome. This is my first stage appearance in this country. I didn't know what to expect, but that greeting was terrific."

And this comment came after a misunderstanding between Gene and his enthusiastic audience, mainly made up of teenage girls, when Gene, after only singing a couple of numbers, paced off the stage as if he didn't intend to come back.

The fans' cheers died. "We want Gene," they chanted. There was a long pause and it seemed he would not return. Several fans shouted angrily and, at last, the singer came back.

"Maybe they thought I had finished my act," Gene said afterwards. "But I just wanted to get off the stage for a while, that's all."

Gene said that from what he had seen of British rock 'n' roll stars—Terry Dene, Vince Eager, Dickie Pride and Johnny Gentle were among those featured with him in The Marty Wilde Show—he thought they were very good.

"They have plenty of rhythm and they all seem excellent showmen," he said. "What's most important, the fans seem to love them."

While he is in this country Gene has been very busy.

"But I'm enjoying every minute of it," he said. "All I hope is I get such a warm reception when I go to Paris and then Germany next week."

Gene can be heard on Radio Luxembourg tomorrow, Friday, in the Capitol programme. Disc jockey Ray Orchard has been with Gene continually since his arrival, taping on the spot events. The interview will conclude with a personal message from Gene to all his British fans.

As stated in DISC last week, Gene Vincent returns to this country in January for a tour of Granada theatres with Al Saxon, Wee Willie Harris, The Bachelors, The Rockets, Lance Fortune and Keith Kelly, with Don Arden compering the show.

The show opens at Maidstone on January 6, then goes to Harrow (7), Dartford (8), Rugby (9), Walthamstow (10), Kingston (11), Aylesbury (12), Bedford (13), Kettering (14), Grantham (15), Mansfield (16) and the Adelphi, Slough (17). In this final concert, Al Saxon will be replaced by Cherry Wainer.

GENE VINCENT (centre) chats to (left to right), Jack Good, Marty Wilde, Joyce Baker, Joe Brown and Little Tony shortly after his arrival in this country last week-end. (DISC Pic).

DISC

THE TOP RECORD & MUSICAL WEEKLY

No. 89   Week ending December 5, 1959

GENE VINCENT

THURSDAY

INSIDE

Amazing 'heart' record

The most fantastic disc ever

Help me choose Gene's songs for his 'B.M.G.' spot

"FIVE Days, Five Days," "Be-Bop-a-Lula," "Bluejean Bop," "Rocky Road Blues," "Say Mama," "Frankie and Johnnie," and so on and so on. It's driving me crazy. I have to decide which of the countless Gene Vincent hits to feature on "Boy Meets Girls" in just over a fortnight's time. And it's very tough making a decision.

There's such a wealth of material to select from—and so many different styles, too. In the early days Gene's songs seemed to me to be very much the same, but for a year or so now, Gene has been succesfully tackling every field of pop music—rock, Country and Western, calypso, blues . . . the lot.

I've been listening to all his LPs, and quite apart from the enormous range they display, I have been struck by the polish with which each track on the more recent Vincent albums has been performed and recorded. Any of them could be released as a single well up to Gene's standard. Of how many British rock stars could this be said ?

Of course, this consistent quality in the current Vincent catalogue makes my selection even more of a headache. So I'd like to ask DISC readers for some help.

LET ME KNOW WHICH OF THE GENE VINCENT SONGS YOU WOULD LIKE TO SEE HIM SING ON "B.M.G." AND I WILL FIX IT SO THAT THE MAJORITY OF YOU ARE HAPPY.

4. VINCENT THE FOURTH
Gene comes to the UK

"Birds fly over the rainbow,
Why then, oh why, can't I?"
('Over The Rainbow', Gene Vincent)

Gene Vincent had no idea how to keep people on his side and by November 1959, this multi-million selling star was reduced to poor quality gigs in the US, using pick-up bands with guitarists and drummers who weren't in the Musicians' Union. It was his own fault but he didn't see it that way and thought that the whole Establishment was against him. He wanted to keep on singing as he hated the idea of jacking it in for a day job.

Enter Norm Riley, a friendly, middle-aged businessman, who called everybody 'Herman'. Riley was always looking for a financial opportunity (for himself). He'd told everyone that he had been in music before, managing Hank Williams, but as the country star was dead, nobody could verify this impressive story and I've yet to come across his name in a Williams biography. He claimed to have booked Elvis Presley in the early days, published Jim Reeves' hits, promoted Fabian concerts and created the illusion that Marvin Rainwater was Cherokee. He knew that Gene was talented and desperate for work, so he thought about Europe and, in particular, the UK. As Gene had had some mental illness, possibly he was manic depressive, Riley acted as his guarantor for his UK appearances.

Jack Good was a 28-year-old TV producer. He had studied at Balliol College, Oxford and had been president of the university's dramatic society (OUDS). He joined the BBC and told them, much to their surprise, that Tommy Steele was as exciting as Olivier. They wanted a youth programme and so he devised and produced their first teenage programme, '6.5 Special'. Soon the executive were objecting to the way he allowed his audience to roam across the studio. Good wanted a programme that was 100% rock'n'roll and when the BBC refused, he switched to one of the ITV companies, ABC, for the fast-moving 'Oh Boy!' which would cram 20 songs into half an hour. He said, "Just as Hollywood's great years were born out of the Depression, rock'n'roll lifted us from the gloomy Fifties. Show-biz thrives when times are low because it enables you to forget what is going on around you."

The BBC was foolish to get rid of Good as he was sympathetic to the new music, a great organiser and someone who knew what teenagers wanted. He also was a star-maker as both Cliff Richard and Marty Wilde had huge successes following regular appearances on 'Oh Boy!'. Nevertheless, the plan to make 'Oh Boy!' popular in the States faltered. The American Broadcasting Company (a completely different ABC) bought filmed recordings of 'Oh Boy!' to show across their network in the States. The public disliked the show and the reviews were abysmal. The 'Journal-American' ran the headline, "British Get Even For 1776" and its reviewer, Jack O'Brien stated, "It has not one lone British mood in its entire 30 minute length." The 'New York Herald Tribune' asked why "an appalling piece of trash like this should return for a second week." Ben Gross in the 'Daily News' showed his contempt for all things rock'n'roll with, "At last England has had her revenge. She exported to these shores a form of torture we have long inflicted on Britain." Although 'Oh Boy!' failed as a summer replacement series, the UK entertainer Dave King did well with his variety show. Although only two 'Oh Boy!' programmes are known to have survived, this suggests that there may be copies of other shows on some storage shelves in America.

In 1959, Jack Good's 'Oh Boy!' show was replaced with 'Boy Meets Girls', a less frenzied programme featuring complete songs and devised as a showcase for Marty Wilde and the Vernons Girls, but still featuring other 'Oh Boy!' performers. The Vernons Girls' musical director, Bill Shepherd, was asked to form a new band for the programme and this became the Firing Squad. He picked 27 musicians but the economics of this proved impossible and by December, Jack Good had reduced it to nine. All the musicians were told to learn their parts and there was to be no sheet music in sight. Saxophonist Red Price, organist Cherry Wainer and drummer Don Storer had survived from the 'Oh Boy!' days. Marty Wilde: "'Boy Meets Girls' was a much tamer version of 'Oh Boy!' but I loved all Jack's shows because I met a lot of terrific people. It was great to work with the Americans. It was marvellous to watch Eddie and Gene and we also had Johnny Cash, Brenda Lee and Freddy Cannon." One of the first guests was Alma Cogan, an indication that the programme didn't really know its market.

Jack Good loathed the rival programme, the static 'Juke Box Jury' and their ridiculous choice of panel members. "The squares on 'Juke Box Jury' would hate the records I like. You can't hear the words and they always think that is the most important thing. They would vote the recording of TIM the biggest hit ever." TIM was the beautifully enunciated speaking clock.

The impresario Larry Parnes was a year older than Jack Good. His father was a wealthy London businessman with a chain of dress shops and Parnes managed two of them. Parnes' real interest was the theatre and he invested in a couple of productions before he too was smitten by Tommy Steele. A friend of his, John Kennedy, had discovered Steele, and Parnes came in with a £100 investment, although he was soon to oust Kennedy from Steele's management. Steele was Parnes' ideal: a hard-working performer who wanted to be an all- round entertainer. By 1959, Steele had all but turned his back on rock'n'roll.

That Tommy Steele kept smiling when he was worked so hard by his manager, Larry Parnes, showed what a trouper he was. Cliff Michelmore asked Parnes on the new 'Tonight' programme in 1957 if Steele was being overworked. Parnes denied it but there is a letter on the BBC's files from Steele's mother thanking him for his question.

Larry Parnes: "Tommy Steele is the prime example of a stage trouper. If a doctor told him that he should take a week off, he would say, 'One night will do. I want to get back on that stage.' Tommy would work through thick and thin and indeed, all my artists were truly dedicated workers."

Parnes was a decisive and divisive man with enormous self-belief. Following his national success with Tommy Steele, he built a stable of stars, as he called it, though he put himself at No.1. His artists had the Parnes brand name. Generally, this was a friendly first name with a tough surname: Tommy Steele, Marty Wilde, Billy Fury, Duffy Power and Vince Eager. It's said that Parnes, a closet gay, named them after how he thought they behaved in the sack, but there is no evidence of this, despite calling one of his charges, Dickie Pride and promoting the South African singer, Dickie Loader. Joe Brown rejected a ridiculous name (Elmer Twitch), although Parnes took revenge by working him astonishingly hard. Parnes never published his autobiography, but 'What's In A Name?' would have been a suitable title.

At the time, Parnes said of his charges, "They go through very extensive grooming. It is sometimes five months before they appear on stage. To start with, they have to have physical grooming. I have their hair cut – that is very important. Sometimes they have bad skin and that has to be attended to. Then I provide them with suitable clothes and some comfort. I like them to live in a good home, get three good meals a day, get to bed early, and have plenty of fresh air." I can only assume that he took on Gene Vincent because he wanted a challenge, and no doubt Vincent often heard his catch-phrase, "I'll be very lucky for you. I'm always lucky for people."

The Liverpool Records Office holds the interview tapes of the late BBC Radio Merseyside presenter, Bob Azurdia. He conducted a 90 minute interview with Parnes in 1988 which is a wonderful example of revisionist history. They had both seen the Liverpool Playhouse musical about the 1960 tour, 'Be Bop A Lula'.

Parnes: "In this show, 'Be Bop A Lula', they mention that I gave certain artists of mine £25 a week or £40 a week. That's true but they didn't mention that I also used to give their mothers' money which was not in the contract. I used to pay their housekeeping. I bought all their clothes, spent money on their travel and put money in the bank for them."

Azurdia: (Incredulous) "All of them?"

Parnes: "Oh yes I did, all of them. I looked after all of them. I started my artists on £25 a week rising every year. You equate that, 30 years later, with now. Surely £40 in 1958 would be £1,200 now."

Azurdia: "The implication in the play is that you did rather better out of it than the artists."

Parnes: "But I didn't. I came out of the pop business with less than I went in. Every penny that I earned in the pop business, in rock'n'roll, I put back into it."

Azurdia: (Even more incredulous) "Every penny you earned?"

Parnes: "Every penny I earned. I needed all the capital: I didn't have backers and I didn't have other people's money. I had my own money. There weren't the backers around that there are now."

Azurdia: "You must have had a separate account for yourself."

Parnes: "Well, I had to eat and I had to have a roof over my head. I didn't live in ultimate luxury. I never had luxurious cars, although I had nice cars, I nearly always had a Vauxhall Cresta that I ran around in. I didn't drive around in Rolls-Royces."

Larry Parnes had discovered the timber yard worker, Marty Wilde, in 1957 and he appeared on '6.5 Special' and then 'Oh Boy!'. He had a Top 10 hit with the 'death disc', 'Endless Sleep' in the summer of 1958 and his version was much more atmospheric than the American original by Jody Reynolds. It led to a brief appearance on the Royal Varity Performance where he performed 'All American Boy', an unlikely choice, to say the least. Marty spent the winter months in 'Babes In The Wood', which was produced by Hughie Green, at the Stockton Hippodrome. In 1959 he had four Top 10 singles with covers of 'Donna', 'A Teenager In Love', 'Sea Of Love' and his own composition, 'Bad Boy'. His album, 'Wilde About Marty', demonstrated his versatility and he appeared with Dame Sybil Thorndike and Harry Secombe in the drama, 'Jet Storm', which was partly shot at London Airport.

Parnes was very keen that Marty Wilde should appeal to a family audience. In his opinion, the kids had four shillings or so on a Saturday and they approached Mum to make up the price of a disc. He told the NME, "This gives Mum a say in the choice and she is apt to say, 'Why don't you buy that nice tune we heard Marty Wilde sing on TV?' This makes Mum - and Dad - a potent force in the record sales and it is worth any artist's while to angle his stuff at them."

Some first generation American rock'n'rollers had toured the UK – Bill Haley and his Comets, Freddie Bell and the Bellboys, Frankie Lymon and the Teenagers, Charlie Gracie, and Buddy Holly and the Crickets – but not many. 1959 had been barren: Lew and Leslie Grade had brought in Connie Francis and Tito Burns had Paul Anka, and, er, that's it. The experiences with Jerry Lee Lewis for the all-powerful Grades may have put off promoters and made them suspicious of Americans. Larry Parnes could see the benefits in rekindling an interest in American rock'n'roll stars and also packing the bill with his own acts, but he knew that they were expensive.

Except Gene Vincent. Gene had created so much havoc in America that he would accept anything that was going.

Larry Parnes: "My dear, wonderful friend Hymie Zahl of Fosters Agency told me that Gene Vincent was available through his manager Norm Riley. I said I was interested and a couple of days later, I was rung up by someone from the Grade Organisation at six in the morning and told, 'You are not to bring this American artist into Britain. Our company has the sole right for all American artists.' They were trying to scare me and they were talking rubbish. They had a lot of control and I couldn't get Eddie or Gene on 'Sunday Night At The London Palladium', for example."

I put Parnes' comments to a fellow impresario, Jeff Kruger: "I tried to get Tony Crombie and the Rockets on 'Sunday Night At The London Palladium' and ran into exactly the same problem as Larry but this was a few years earlier. It wasn't that the Grades disliked Larry bringing in American stars, but rather that the Grades disliked Larry as someone who might, in some small way, threaten their position. That says a lot for the frailty of Lew Grade's ego, who was impossible to deal with. In the end, I broke through because of my friendship with Leslie Grade and the respect that Bernard Delfont showed me, but Lew was impossible to deal with."

Whenever his budget permitted, Jack Good used American performers in his TV programmes. He had used Brenda Lee, Conway Twitty and Johnny Cash, and he was delighted to hear from Norm Riley that Gene Vincent was available. To spread the cost, he had to see whether Larry Parnes could use him. It is said that Larry Parnes was so impressed when he saw Gene on 'Boy Meets Girls' that he signed him for a UK tour in January, but things don't happen that fast, especially in 1959, with Christmas on the way and work permits to be resolved. ATV would have obtained a working visa reasonably easily as he would be classified as a solo variety entertainer, rather than a musician. If this were the case, Larry Parnes could capitalise on the situation and add him to a package tour of British artists, which he had already set up.

Gene Vincent was well served by Capitol Records in the UK as the label, which was affiliated to EMI, released a stream of wonderful singles. This is despite the fact that they didn't sell in any great quantities. Even 'Be Bop A Lula' only reached No.16 in the UK. This was followed by 'Race With The Devil' (28), and 'Bluejean Bop' (16). There had been 13 subsequent singles but they had only been bought by the keenest fans. What's more, Capitol had issued five albums – 'Bluejean Bop' (1956), 'Gene Vincent And The Blue Caps' (1957), 'Gene Vincent Rocks And The Blue Caps Roll' (1958), 'A Gene Vincent Record Date' (1958) and 'Sounds Like Gene Vincent' (1959). Even in the midst of his problems, Gene Vincent was still recording good music – a new album, 'Crazy Times', was ready for release - and Capitol was persevering with him. Maybe Capitol recognised that he was the one great *bona fide* rock'n'roller that they had on their books or maybe they just felt sorry for him.

The various strands – Norm Riley, Jack Good, Larry Parnes and Capitol Records in the UK – were brought together, and Gene Vincent flew into London Airport (now Heathrow) on Saturday 5 December 1959. He arrived at 7am and many fans were there to welcome him. Gene hadn't wanted to draw attention to himself. Pistol packin' Vincent liked to carry a gun and a knife and he had strapped them to his leg-iron so that they would not be identified by the metal detector.

Jack Good: "I remember it was dark and London Airport was just a bunch of hangars. The plane landed and Gene Vincent came down the steps. He was a quiet, thin, wan fellow in a baseball jacket, and he said, 'Hello, sir, I'm happy to make your acquaintance.' I thought this will never do – he's got to be a rocker. He's got to say, 'Hey, man, what's happening?' I was deeply disturbed and I wondered what we were going to do. From his records, I thought he was going to be a dagger boy, the rock'n'roll Screaming End, and here was a polite man from Virginia. I'd have to fix him." Jack Good had no idea that the dagger was already there.

Once through Customs, Gene met his fans, while Joe Brown and his skiffle group, the Spacemen, had assembled to play him into the UK. Gene was interviewed by the Canadian disc-jockey, Ray Orchard, who worked on Radio Luxembourg and played the result on his sponsored programme for Capitol product. Gene says very little – Orchard's questions are longer than the replies but he reveals that he has a farm outside New Orleans. I think not.

Gene was driven to Broadcasting House for a live interview on the Light Programme's 'Saturday Club' with its host, Brian Matthew. The fee for this three minute interview was 5 guineas, which was paid in dollars. Because Gene had a contract with ABC-TV, Brian Matthew was supposed to mention that he would be appearing on 'Boy Meets Girls'. Gene could have brought this up, but he didn't. Neither 'Boy Meets Girls' nor ABC were mentioned and the agent Hymie Zahl exploded and wrote to the BBC about this on 11 December: "They (ABC-TV)are not asking for damages from the BBC or from us, but they informed me that they felt Gene Vincent had breached his contract and they were considering whether they would deduct anything from his contract. I must ask you please if you cannot cooperate with us on these artists, that they just cannot go on your show, and I would be most grateful if you would please let me know why this matter was not mentioned." An internal note says that they hope ABC does not consider the BBC in breach of contract and that they admit to be more to blame than Vincent.

Vincent checked in at his hotel and attended a reception at the Bagatelle Club in Mayfair, where he met Marty Wilde, Joyce Baker from the Vernons

Girls (whom Marty had just married), Joe Brown once again and an Italian rock'n'roller based in the UK, Little Tony. Once again, he displayed his southern cordiality by calling everybody 'Sir' or 'Ma'am'. This wasn't super-politeness but a reflex response on Gene's part and though few in the UK knew it, millions of Americans from the South behaved in the same way, Elvis Presley among them.

The next day Gene went to the Granada Theatre in Tooting and like many of the Granada cinemas, it was converted to a theatre for the occasional concert. They had rooms round the back that could be used as dressing-rooms so the conditions weren't too bad. This was the biggest Granada in the UK, seating 3,000 customers. Johnny Hamp had been the manager in charge and then he became the booking manager for the 30 cinemas in the Granada chain. Hamp would later produce a memorable TV special for Gene Vincent.

Gene Vincent worked through five songs with Joe Brown and some of Larry Parnes' musicians. A year earlier, it had been the third and final location for the Jerry Lee Lewis tour, which was then cancelled by Leslie Grade. Jerry Lee had married his 13-year-old second cousin and the country was in an uproar. Dylan may have been chastened by shouts of "Judas" but it was far worse for Lewis, who suffered the cries of "Cradle-robber".

Gene Vincent was treated like a hero when he was the special guest on 'The Marty Wilde Show'. The bill was packed with Parnes' artists - Billy Fury, Vince Eager, Duffy Power, Johnny Gentle, Dickie Pride, Julian X (Parnes running out of ideas) as well as the only filly in his stable, the singer and pianist Sally Kelly.

The performances were a microcosm of Gene Vincent. During the first house, he left the stage without explanation after two numbers. The fans shouted "We want Gene" and he returned and completed his set. At the second house, he had some microphone trouble but his microphone was changed and all was well.

Most of the artists on the bill wore drainpipe trousers but Gene wore baggy, black trousers, which hid his leg-iron and also was an American fashion that had not reached the UK. Although he did not have black leathers and was wearing a red and black sweater, he had many of the movements that are associated with him. He had a curious, half-crouching stance over the microphone stand, which was about three feet high. He raised the stand above his head before bringing it to the ground and swinging his bad leg over the top. Although he might announce a song to the audience, he never looked at them: he was always staring into the distance.

Marty Wilde was making his first appearance as a married man but he had no cause to worry as the fans liked him singing, "Why must I be a teenager in love?" Marty Wilde recalls, "For some stupid reason, Larry wanted me to top the bill and I thought, prior to the show, that it was crazy as Gene had never appeared here before. I should have closed the first half, with Gene closing the show. It would be like me having hits in America and never going there – one day I go and I'd be bound to beat the local artists. I did struggle for the first couple of numbers but I got them in the end and I thought, 'Oh god, I hope that doesn't happen again.'"

The reviews of the show were mixed. 'Disc' loved it, but as Jack Good was writing the review, it was hardly unbiased: "Gene is no sex bomb. He neither uses nor needs any of the suggestive moments that are usually associated with the stage performances of star rockers. Vincent is a man's man, a tough guy. He is rock'n'roll's James Cagney and it is for this reason that an unusually large proportion of his fan club consists of boys. When I say Gene uses no sexy movements, do not think that he does not move on stage. He moves all right. And visually, it is the most unusual rock presentation I have ever witnessed. He crouches with the mike almost throughout the act. He has to, since he keeps it at a height of two feet six inches. He spins, throws and catches the mike, and swings his leg over it in a single short burst of movement. Then, like a crouching tiger awaiting its prey, he will be stock still for minutes on end."

Good had already sussed that Gene was a Jekyll and Hyde character – quiet and shy off-stage and wild in performance, although the two divisions were not as sharply defined as that and Gene at times was more a Hyde and Hyde character. Although Gene Vincent's records were bathed in echo, Good was delighted (and no doubt relieved) to discover that he had a fine singing voice without any embellishments. Norman Heath in 'Melody Maker' was less kind. He said Vincent "might just as well have stayed at home. Admittedly, he was no worse than most of the home-grown rockers, but he was certainly no better."

The following week Jack Good got to know Gene Vincent as he rehearsed with the so-called Firing Squad for appearances on 'Boy Meets Girls' at the television studios in Didsbury in south Manchester. The Firing Squad featured many of the UK's finest musicians: Joe Brown (lead guitar), Brian Daly and Eric Ford (rhythm guitar), Red Price (tenor sax), Cherry Wainer (organ), Alan Weighall (electric bass), Bill Stark (double-bass), and Don Storer and Andy White (drums). The Vernons Girls were called upon for backing vocals or screams as appropriate. Although it was never broadcast, Gene had a jam session with Cliff Richard and the Shadows.

Jack Good was tremendously excited to be working with an American performer and even more so as he planned to change his presentation. His productions for OUDS came in useful: "Gene Vincent had a leg iron, so he hobbled a bit. I was a Shakespeare fan, so hobbling to me meant Richard III. I even thought of giving him a hunchback, and I'm glad I didn't! Then I thought, 'He can also be moody like Hamlet', so we'll dress him in black from head to toe and put a medallion round his neck. I once played a murderer, Lightbourne, with gloves on, which was very sinister, so I added that."

I asked Jack Good if he told Gene where his ideas came from, but he told me not to be silly. "Oh no, I don't think he'd ever heard of Shakespeare. I never talked to him about that. I simply said, 'This is what you're wearing' and he just did anything I told him. It was 'Yes, sir', 'Yes, sir' all the time. I arranged to have some steps on 'Boy Meets Girls' so that he could hobble nicely, but he negotiated them very well, and hardly looked as if he was hobbling at all. I had to yell out, 'Limp, you bastard, limp.' He didn't mind: he limped."

Joe Brown dismisses the Shakespearean origins: "I wore black leather all the time because I had a motorbike. Jack could have got the idea from me. I don't lay claim to it, but I've got a feeling it was."

On Saturday teatime, 12 December 1959, Gene Vincent made his first live appearance on a UK TV programme. At one point, Gene went into the wrong song but the band picked up on it okay. The 'Boy Meets Girls' appearance was a success which was just as well as two further appearances had been recorded the day before. Hence, Gene was also on 'Boy Meets Girls' on 19 December and Boxing Day. Jack Good had asked 'Disc' readers to vote on the song that they would like Gene to perform on 'Boy Meets Girls' and Gene obliged by performing his sinuous, Latin-styled 'Summertime', which he sang in a delicate falsetto. As well as 'Summertime', the numbers he performed on the three appearances were 'Be Bop A Lula', 'Bluejean Bop', 'Say Mama', 'Baby Blue', 'Five Days. Five Days', 'I Got A Baby', 'Rocky Road Blues', 'Frankie And Johnny' and both sides of his current single, 'Wild Cat' (how apt!) and 'Right Here On Earth'. 'Wild Cat' started to sell and it did make the Top 30 in January. The most memorable performance was the slow and burning 'Baby Blue'.

A well satisfied Gene Vincent told the NME's Derek Johnson: "The main difference is that the British try to achieve perfection. In the States, they just put you in front of a camera, and tell you to sing."

The recordings which have survived (audio only and inferior sound quality) are very competent. In interviews, Gene said that he had been apprehensive about the quality of British musicians, but he could see that Joe Brown and Red Price were world class. The ferocity of Joe Brown's playing in 'Rocky Road Blues' rivals the Americans and nobody hearing the sessions would think that Brits couldn't play rock'n'roll: they had risen to the challenge.

And the arrangements hadn't spoilt Gene's voice in any way. Graham Fenton of Matchbox: "Some of the rock'n'rollers had rough, raunchy voices but Gene had this pure golden voice - nobody else was singing like him. Gene was an original and apart from the echo, he wasn't trying to be Elvis. He had his own voice, his own songs and his own style."

Larry Parnes played snakes and ladders with his artists and the winning square was being accepted as an all-round entertainer. His first star, Tommy Steele, had outgrown rock'n'roll and was making major strides in this direction. He had a successful film with the comedy, 'Tommy The Toredor', with Sidney James and the hit song, 'Little White Bull' and early in 1960, he was to star alongside Peggy Mount in 'She Stoops To Conquer' at the Old Vic. Parnes saw a similar career path for Marty Wilde and in January 1960, he signed a £100,000 two-year deal for Marty with the impresario Harold Fielding and the agent Ian Bevan, who had similar associations with Tommy Steele. Wilde would continue to be managed by Parnes but there would be more films than touring packages in future. Because Parnes had these plans for Marty Wilde, he thought that he could put Gene with Marty's group, the Wildcats, to good effect.

Gene left the UK for appearances in France and Germany, firstly at the Paris Olympia on December 15. The co-promoter, Lucien Morisse was a director of the radio station, Europe No.1 and like other promotions, he planned to record and broadcast the concert. Gene worked with a small orchestra that the station provided and one of the highlights was his performance of an Otis Blackwell rockabilly song, 'It's No Lie'. The concert was broadcast on 30 December 1959 but no tapes have surfaced. It is sometimes thought that Gene was uncomfortable with the image that Jack Good had created but the photographs from the Paris Olympia show him in black leather. He was mobbed after his performance and his jacket was torn. He went from Paris to concerts in Frankfurt and played some American bases. In an interview with Gene in the Christmas edition of 'Melody Maker', Gene said that he was planning to stay in the UK until October 1960. Gene always spoke twaddle in interviews, but maybe this was true. Quite how Parnes was going to clear this with the authorities wasn't clear, but he was already organising a five week tour, starting in January, and he wanted Gene for a summer season, either in Blackpool or Great Yarmouth.

A summer season in Blackpool may not be everybody's idea of heaven but Gene Vincent had been thrown a lifeline. He had been on his best behaviour and he knew that he mustn't mess it up. He hadn't used his weapons and hadn't taken the name, the Firing Squad, as an invitation. He was the model tourist: he didn't quite say your policemen are wonderful, but he wanted to see the Changing of the Guard.

GENE MEETS MARTY

GENE VINCENT got a warm welcome to Britain last week. He met many stars at his reception where the picture above was taken, showing (l to r) MARTY and JOYCE WILDE, GENE, and LITTLE TONY.

Gene Vincent : 40 performances in major cities

AMERICAN rock 'n' roll star, Gene Vincent is to headline a package show for a nation-wide, five-week, one-night-stand tour starting at the end of January—his first engagement under a contract signed with impresario Larry Parnes.

Commencing on January 23, after his tour of Granada theatres, Vincent will play four twice-nightly shows in major cities each week. Vince Eager leads the supporting bill, which includes Sally Kelly, Billy Raymond and The Tony Sheridan Trio.

To follow the one-nighters, Parnes plans to arrange three weeks in variety for Gene and is currently working on a plan to present him in a resident summer season show if Vincent is able to prolong his stay.

Early in the New Year, Parnes will fly to America with Hyman Zahl, of Fosters Agency, to sign other top rock stars for British appearances. He also hopes to arrange tours in the U.S. for his own artists.

"Good Health!" say Marty Wilde, Little Tony and Gene Vincent with a Christmas toast to NME readers.

Gene sings 'Summertime'

MY request that DISC readers should suggest which numbers they would like Gene Vincent to sing on "Boy Meets Girls" was very interesting. One number almost everyone plumped for was Gene's version of "Summertime," so we will be doing that one on the first show.

Here are the other titles we will be featuring: "Baby Blue," "I Gotta Baby," "Right Here On Earth" and "Wild Cat" (his latest record), "Rocky Road Blues," "Frankie And Johnnie," "Blue Jean Bop," "Five Days," "Say Mama" and "Be-Bop-A-Lula."

GENE VINCENT

WITH HIS SPECIAL REQUEST DISC

'Summertime' b/w 'Frankie and Johnnie'
45—CL15035

GENE VINCENT and JOE BROWN whip up a storm on the Boxing Day "Boy Meets Girls" show.

GENE VINCENT
Frankie And Johnnie; Summertime
(Capitol CL15035)★★★★

GENE VINCENT trots out his own adaptation of the classic Frankie And Johnnie, bringing the lyrics up to date.

Vincent chants it to a lolloping beat with the Blue Caps supplying a twangy rhythmic accompaniment and adding hand-claps. One the juke crews will enjoy and one which ought to do Vincent plenty of good in this country.

Latterly the boy's been proving that he's more versatile than many of us originally gave him credit for being. Listen to his Latin-tempoed treatment of the Gershwin number, Summertime. Purists who like their "Porgy and Bess" in the original may object —but I think this is an intelligent adaptation which deserves to succeed.

Gene Vincent makes British debut with Marty Wilde and 'Beat Show' gang

Terry Dene

Larry Parnes' vocal line-up at the Tooting Granada on Sunday was (l to r): DICKIE PRIDE, BILLY FURY, VINCE EAGER, JULIAN, MARTY WILDE, DUFFY POWER and JOHNNY GENTLE.

WEARING a red-and-black sweater, and jet black trousers, Gene Vincent made his first appearance in this country at Tooting Granada on Sunday in front of a capacity audience.

Gene closed the first half of the all-rock show with a performance that put him way above the rest of the artists in stagecraft and showmanship.

In spite of an injury sustained in a car smash some years ago which left him slightly lame, Vincent performed miracles with the stand mike he used throughout his performance. He hoisted it above his head, swung his leg over the top of it, and generally made a very heavy prop look like featherweight bamboo cane!

Add a peculiar, half-crouching stance, and his act was not only good to listen to, it was well worth watching, too!

Most of the numbers he sang were new to British ears, but all Vincent fans knew his first hit "Be Bop A Lula," which was extremely well received.

Unfortunately, Gene and his backing group, led by guitarist Joe Brown, hadn't been able to have sufficient rehearsal. This was noticeable, but it didn't make a great deal of difference to Gene's memorable performance. But it could have made it even better.

After the show, many fans gathered at the stage door yelling for Gene, hammering on the door and showing that his first visit is certainly no disappointment to the fans who have heard him only on disc.

The rest of the package was the complete Larry Parnes' "Beat Show," including Marty Wilde (making his first theatre-appearance as a married man), Billy Fury, Duffy Power, Sally Kelly, Vince Eager, Dickie Pride, Johnny Gentle, Julian X, Terry Dene and The Viscounts.

Marty, of course, had the Granada reverberating with screams when he came on stage singing "Mack The Knife."

"Teenager In Love," "Donna," "Sea Of Love" and his latest chart entry "Bad Boy" made up the rest of his act.

Billy Fury also had his fair share of the screams and Vince Eager's powerful versions of "Make Believe" and "What Do You Want To Make Those Eyes At Me For?" earned the appreciation of a full-house.

New addition to the Parnes stable, Julian X, has an attractive voice and stands more or less motionless when he sings. Maybe he's trying to evolve a new style or perhaps he's just nervous.

Incidentally, this package, minus Gene Vincent and Marty Wilde, starts a week's variety at London's Finsbury Park Empire on Monday.

The Viscounts

Beat Boys; Red Reece, Georgie Fame, Gene, Billy (Ray) McVay, Vince Cooze and Colin Green

5. STRANGER ON THE SHORE
Gene's first UK tour

"Why oh why must I go on like this,
Shall I be just a lonely stranger on the shore?"
('Stranger On The Shore', the Drifters)

Larry Parnes had put together 'The Be-Bop-A-Lula Tour' for 12 days in January 1960. Nothing wrong with Gene at the top of the bill, but the rest of the content was decidedly cheapskate. Wee Willie Harris had been comical enough on '6.5 Special', but the jokes had faded and although he could be a decent rock'n'roll and blues singer, nobody took him seriously. Al Saxon had made the Top 20 with 'You're The Top Cha', which gave Cole Porter's song a glossy Bobby Darin-styled treatment. His cover of Sam Cooke's 'Only Sixteen' had been nowhere near as successful as Craig Douglas's. As he was not available for the January 17 booking, he was replaced by Cherry Wainer.

Both Lance Fortune and Keith Kelly had yet to have any hits, and Lance's first single, 'Be Mine' was issued on January 30. Richard Keen and Rikki Gavin were a duo called the Bachelors, who made 'Please Don't Touch' for Parlophone in 1959. Although they were produced by George Martin, their singles failed to sell and, in two years' time, a Dublin trio used the same name and had several international hits. Intriguingly, Parnes had booked the entertainer Don Arden as compère. You could laugh with Don Arden but never at him.

The road manager for the tour was a Liverpudlian Hal Carter. He had helped Larry Parnes get Marty Wilde in and out of the Liverpool Empire in 1958 and Parnes was impressed by his skill. He offered him a job at £10 a week. "I was a foreman at Union Carbide on £18 a week but this was show-biz," said Carter. He was exceptionally good at his job and particularly skilful at keeping fans at bay.

Wee Willie Harris recalls, "Gene was very quiet and shy but he came out of his shell once you got to know him. He called me 'Sir' at first but I told him to call me 'Willie'. He thought I was crazy with my pink hair. He'd say, 'I don't know how you got the nerve to go on stage like that.'" Lance Fortune has a similar memory: "He was a Southern gentleman and he would say 'Yes, sir' and 'No, sir' to anyone, even me. He was like that...until you got to know him." Note the ominous tones in both those quotes.

As if to add some culture to their lives, Jack Good suggested that Gene and Wee Willie Harris went to a ballet at the Royal Festival Hall. Gene also went to see the West End musical, 'When In Rome' starring Dickie Henderson and June Laverick. Gene wasn't used to using stage make-up in America but once he had seen others using it, he started applying it himself.

True to form, Gene had not had his leather jacket repaired or bought a new one. Instead, he did the performances in a variety of outfits: sometimes in what he happened to be wearing during the day. In the States, he had sometimes worn a vivid green suit with 'GV' on the breast pocket. It was rather like a safari jacket with trousers. He wore this on occasion but it looked comical and detracted from the music, turning him into a rock'n'roll leprechaun.

Gene Vincent gave half-hour sets, often closing with 'Be-Bop-A-Lula' and repeating it for the encore. Well, it was 'The Be-Bop-A-Lula Tour'. The familiar material was there but he also included 'Brand New Beat' and his ballad, 'Important Words'. The show itself would always close with the National Anthem, which was a brilliant way of clearing the theatre as patrons would try and leave before it started as otherwise, they would have to remain dutifully on the spot, an indication of how passive most teenagers were back then.

In the States, Gene used to watch television non-stop, all night if the monster movies were on. He was surprised to find that Britain only had black and white TV and that it closed down at 11pm. It made him irritable and like Don Arden, Gene was not the sort of person that you could joke with as it could easily rebound on you. A later road manager, Henry Henroid, recalled, "Gene used to start books, often weird science-fiction ones, but I never saw him finish anything. He didn't laugh very much and when he did, it was nonsense. He would laugh at something very silly."

Meanwhile, Norm Riley had been talking to Jack Good about further American performers for 'Boy Meets Girls'. He had made contact with Eddie Cochran and Ronnie Hawkins. Eddie Cochran seemed a good choice: he looked great and he had done better than Gene Vincent in the UK charts with three Top 30 hits – 'Summertime Blues' (18, 1958), 'C'mon Everybody' (6, 1959) and 'Somethin' Else' (22, 1959). His latest release was a beaty version of Ray Charles' 'Hallelujah I Love Her So' and the American teen magazines suggested that Eddie was singing it to his baby, the actress Connie Stevens.

On Friday 8 January 1960, Eddie Cochran recorded at the Goldstar Studios in Hollywood. He was working with Sonny Curtis and Jerry Allison of the Crickets as well as his usual bass player, Guybo Smith. Here was Cochran, terrified of flying since Buddy Holly's death, working with two of Holly's musicians and about to fly across the Atlantic. They were recording two songs that would hold additional meaning if anything happened to him – 'Three Steps To Heaven' (written with his brother Bob) and 'Cherished Memories' (a Sharon Sheeley song). It was a productive session as the third song was the country novelty, 'Cut Across Shorty'. The girl in the song has made up her mind that Shorty is for her, a choice which would have appealed to Cochran, who wished he was that little bit taller – he was five foot six. He had small hands and his shoes were only size 4.

On that same day, Billy Fury was recording his own song, 'Collette', at the Decca studios in London. It was strongly influenced by the Everly Brothers and Billy harmonised with one of the Vernons Girls, Ann O'Brien. Joe Brown was playing guitar and the single, which was produced by Jack Good, was very pleasant and commercial. It was released at the end of the month and gave Billy his first Top 10 hit, peaking at No.9 in 'Record Retailer', although it only reached No.19 on the NME chart.

Eddie had hoped to bring over the band, the Kelly Four, to back him but the Musicians' Union would not allow this. This was a legacy from earlier decades where there had been a ban on American musicians working in the UK. The ban had only recently been relaxed but it was still far easier for a singer to work in the UK than an accompanying musician.

The day before Eddie arrived in the UK, David Jacobs played the B-side of his latest single, that is, 'Little Angel' instead of 'Hallelujah I Love Her So' on 'Juke Box Jury'. 'Little Angel' was a rough-edged, medium-tempo doo-wop song, a good performance but not one that the panel – Gilbert Harding, actress Shirley Anne Field, songwriter Lionel Bart and Anita Pryne (no idea who this was and neither has Google) – would endorse. Why was this track selected? I can only assume it was sabotage: the BBC knew that Cochran would be on ITV's teenage programme for Saturday teatime, 'Boy Meets Girls' and they wanted to demonstrate that Cochran wasn't worth hearing. Whatever, it backfired as Gilbert Harding, probably out of sheer obstinacy, declared his love for the record. David Jacobs was so astonished that he gave Gilbert the BBC's copy, so clearly DJ as a DJ wasn't going to be playing it again.

Also on 8 January the BBC was approached about Gene and Eddie appearing on 'Saturday Club'. They had been forgiven for the *faux pas* in December and were keen to pursue this.

Eddie arrived in London on Sunday 10 January and the following day, Decca, which released his records in the UK on the London-American label, held a press reception. A photographer took that well-known picture of him calling home and putting a finger to his lips to ask for quiet. The film reviewer Peter Haigh, 'Oh Boy!' compère, Tony Hall as well as Billy Fury, Joe Brown, Terry Dene and Jack Good were at the reception, and Eddie sang an acoustic 'Hallelujah I Love Her So'.

Brian Gregg, who played bass for Terry Dene, told me, "While Larry Parnes was talking to Terry, Eddie leaned over to me, nodded towards Larry and said, 'Hey, is this guy a fag?' I didn't know what he meant at first as, to us, a fag was a cigarette, but I soon caught on and told him, yes, he was. Eddie leaned behind my back and said to Gene, 'I told you, Gene, the guy's a faggot.'"

Terry Dene: "The American sound was so prevalent in England but we were only copying whereas they were the real thing. I remember having an amusing conversation with them in which I was singing, 'Well, bless my soul, what's wrong with me?' in different British accents."

The similarity in looks between Eddie Cochran and Billy Fury had comic overtones. Larry Parnes often worked in tandem with the agent Hymie Zahl from Foster's Agency. Zahl was short-sighted and wore spectacles that looked like the bottom of bottles. He walked over to Billy Fury and said, "Hello, Eddie, it's good to meet you." Billy Fury was very shy and didn't want to correct him. When Zahl spotted Eddie, he said, "Hello, Billy, how are you?" and gave him a cuddle.

On 12 and 13 January, Eddie had rehearsals in London for 'Boy Meets Girls' and then travelled to Manchester for further rehearsals. Harry Croft interviewed Eddie for 'Manchester Evening News'. Jack Good realised that he didn't need to create a new image for Eddie Cochran: everything was just right. He had to ensure that he caught him at the best camera angles. Sometimes he shot him from below, thus giving the impression that he was taller than he was. Eddie praised Jack Good and thought that his stage act improved considerably because of him.

Marty Wilde: "The first thing I noticed about Eddie was his complexion. We British lads had acne and all the usual problems, and Eddie walked in with the most beautiful hair and the most beautiful skin - his skin was a light brown, beautiful colour, all that California sunshine, and I thought, 'You lucky devil.' We had Manchester white all over us. And he had the most beautiful face - the photographs never did the guy justice. He didn't like our cold weather and I know he was singing 'California Here I Come' in the car when he died. He wanted to get back to that sunshine."

Both Eddie and Gene hated miming and they loved doing live rock'n'roll. Eddie appeared live on 'Boy Meets Girls' on Saturday 16 January and he had also recorded an appearance for the following week. On both shows, he performed the new single, 'Hallelujah I Love Her So', and on the first, he also sang 'C'mon Everybody', 'Somethin' Else' and 'Twenty Flight Rock' and on the second, 'Money Honey' and 'Have I Told You Lately That I Love You'. He was backed by the usual suspects (Joe Brown, Eric Ford, Brian Daley, Red Price, Alan Weighall, Bill Stark, Andy White, Don Storer, Vernons Girls) and Jack Good had time to dub some strings for the second appearance. Eddie was taught some dirty words to 'Money Honey' by a trio of Liverpool singers – Billy Fury, Johnny Gentle, Michael Cox – but he thought twice about using them.

Joe Brown: "I rate Eddie Cochran very highly as a rock'n'roll guitarist. He was great. He could play a good lead guitar but he said, 'Oh, you can play the lead. I'll play rhythm.' Eddie used to play rhythm on stage and he hardly took any solos. He was brilliant. He had an old Selmer amp which we wouldn't use because we didn't think they were any good. We had Vox AC-30s 'cause no-one could get hold of Fenders in those days. He used this old amp and he got a great sound from it, a sound nobody else could get, perhaps because he used a Gretsch guitar and we didn't have them over here."

Gene Vincent's tour finished in Slough on Sunday 17 January and so they had the week for rehearsals before they toured together. Although Parnes was parsimonious, he knew he had to pay for Vincent and Cochran. He didn't pay them direct. Parnes paid Hymie Zahl of Foster's Agency, who took his cut and then paid Norm Riley. I know from documentation that Buddy Holly and the Crickets were receiving $4,000 a week from Lew and Leslie Grade for their UK tour in 1958.

Gene Vincent was top of Larry Parnes' bill and at a rough guess, he was earning $2,500 a week (though most of it was going Norm Riley's way) while Eddie Cochran was known to be on $1,000 (ditto), and there were about $3 to the £. Billy Fury was simply given £20 a week spending money. I haven't found the documentation for Gene's fees but a letter to the Aliens Department from Fosters' Agency dated 9 February 1960 asked for Cochran's Labour Permit to be extended for a further seven weeks to include the booking up to April. It said that all his engagements were at $1,000 a week. This in itself is an unusual letter as the tour dates to mid-April had already been announced.

Norm Riley told 'Disc' on 27 February 1960: "I was sure the tour would be successful, but it was 18 months before I could get a guarantee. Then Larry Parnes stepped in. The result? Fabulous business – at almost £1,000 a night – in Glasgow, Ipswich, Bradford, Southampton, Coventry and Sheffield." The box office receipts are about right but was Riley really suggesting that he had devised this package around July 1958? Another fantasist.

Payola (play for pay) was rife in the US and the issue was being investigated in the UK. Nothing was proved and Reginald Bevin, the Postmaster General, described the UK disc-jockeys as "men of honour". However, although it is not payola, it is possible that Jack Good was close to breaching the guidelines. He was producing a TV show and his main guests were being managed and sent on tour by Larry Parnes. In addition, he would be recommending the artists in his column in 'Disc'. Good would often be producing the artists on record, publishing their songs and acting as a consultant on the staging of the tours. This carries on today on a far more elaborate scale whereby Simon Cowell's company, SyCo, makes the talent shows which are shown on ITV and the winners have a management contract with SyCo and record and tour for him. No rules are being broken but there is no independence – and it stems from Jack Good.

Eddie Cochran would be backed by Marty Wilde's Wildcats (Tony

Belcher, Big Jim Sullivan, Licorice Locking, Brian Bennett) and Gene would use the Beat Boys (Colin Green, Georgie Fame, Vince Cooze, Red Reece, Billy – now Ray – McVay). Eddie would close the first half and Gene would close the show. The supporting acts were Vince Eager and the Quiet Three (who was popular through the BBC's 'Drumbeat'), the Tony Sheridan Trio (who had been on 'Oh Boy!'), the Viscounts (a vocal harmony trio from Morton Fraser's Harmonica Gang) and a 29-year-old compère from Paisley, Billy Raymond who had a strong Scottish accent.

Vince Eager had been born Roy Taylor and Parnes had chosen his new surname, Eager. He had allowed Taylor to choose his own first name and thinking of Gene Vincent, he had picked "Vince". He had an on/off relationship with Larry Parnes: when Vince wondered why he had never received any record royalties, Parnes told him, "You're not entitled to any." Vince protested that he had signed a contract with Top Rank. "Maybe," said Parnes, "but I have power of attorney over you, and I've decided you're not getting any."

Georgie Fame: "We were all told to report to this club in Soho to meet them. I remember Eddie playing guitar and we were astounded. Apart from his own stuff, he could do all that brilliant finger-style stuff that Chet Atkins did. We were sitting around wondering what was next and he played this amazing intro to 'What'd I Say' and everybody said, 'What's that?' Apart from a few blues enthusiasts who had the Ray Charles record, nobody had heard it before. Within six months, every band in the country was playing it."

Eddie's mastery of Chet Atkins' technique meant that he could play both melody and rhythm at the same time, something that none of them had seen before. Tony Sheridan: "Eddie Cochran was from a different environment. He was real and I was a copy. He was a very good guitarist and he was into all sorts of things, which influenced his music. Instead of a third string, he used a second string that he could bend, which was a very clever move. He might suddenly decide to do something differently and that is when something innovative can happen. Gene Vincent was very good but I really learnt things from Eddie."

Effectively, the stage show was produced by Jack Good: "I rehearsed all the singers as though they were actors. They knew what they wanted to do and I tried to give them a look, to help them do it in the most effective way." In Gene's case, Jack Good had devised a whole new routine, but Cochran had it pretty much there from the start. Good wanted an arresting opening and he suggested that Cochran used Ray Charles' 'What'd I Say'. He and the other guitarists could have their backs to the audience as the curtain opened. The riff would build in excitement and then Eddie would turn round for the opening line of the song: "Hey, mama, don't you treat me wrong."

Brian Bennett: "Jack Good was full of energy and he would always praise you if you did something well. Most agents and producers thought that rock'n'roll would last a few years and then it would be back to dance bands again. Jack didn't believe that for one minute. When I first met him, I'd been a jazz musician in a button-down suit and I looked very cool. He'd say to me, 'Brian, for Christ's sake, smile. Smile and make it look difficult.' It's actually pretty hard to smile and make it look difficult. These days people grimace when they play the drums but there was none of that then."

Good, unlike Parnes, hated the concept of turning rock'n'rollers into all-round entertainers, and loathed it when the artists agreed, such as Cliff Richard doing 'Living Doll'. He said, "Nobody expects Bruce Forsyth to appear on 'Boy Meets Girls' and sing 'Mean Woman Blues', so why should young rock stars have to appear in spectaculars and try to be young Fred Astaires?"

Gene's wife, Darlene, flew over with her daughter, Debbie and their own child, Melody, and stayed with Gene in a flat near Piccadilly Circus. Darlene didn't care for the flat and she preferred to go on the road with the children. Everyone remembers her as being quiet and pleasant although her relationship with Gene was volatile. Later on, Gene was given a flat in Fulham.

Music writer Johnny Rogan: "Of course Parnes can be criticised on several counts, but even his critics concede that he was a great manager. He groomed young lads and transformed them from gauche teenagers to mini-stars. He brought the package tour system to the UK by using his own artists, and supplementing the bills with American artists like Eddie and Gene. The tours were sell-outs and were also great experience for the British performers. Joe Brown, Georgie Fame and Billy Fury never forgot their time with Eddie and Gene and that probably applies to everyone on the bill."

Norm Riley had also recommended Ronnie Hawkins, known as 'Mr Dynamo', to Jack Good and he brought him over with his drummer, Levon Helm, for appearances on 'Boy Meets Girls', which were shown on January 30 and February 6. Ever a practical joker, Riley told Hawkins that the sleeper from Manchester to London then went non-stop to Queensland, Australia, so he must leave the train quickly at London. Hawkins did this and according to Riley, he saw the funny side of it. Hawkins did a photo-call with the actress Diana Dors, and Larry Parnes offered him a UK tour. However, Norm Riley had some plans to put Ronnie Hawkins into films and Hawkins now wishes he had done the tour: "Norm Riley promised three billion things and not one of them came through."

Just before the tour started, there was a party at Larry Parnes' flat near Marble Arch. Brian Gregg: "Gene was well away and all of a sudden I heard a crash and he was lying on the floor behind a settee. Eddie said, 'Oh, he'll be okay. Just leave him. If you try and wake him, he'll be vindictive."

Keith Goodwin: "The NME was very definitely the most important paper when it came to rock'n'roll and it kept abreast of the times. I would never have written about their drinking in the NME because there was no heavy-voiced criticism in those days. I thought Vincent was a complete weirdo from the moment I met him. He wanted to be a rebel even if he wasn't one at heart. When I got to know him, I found him a thoroughly nice bloke. Cochran was the very very all-American kid. He used to call me 'Sir' which used to annoy me intensely. I told him that Buddy Holly also called me 'Sir' and it made me feel about 107."

And what did they think of the pieces that Keith wrote about them? "Oh, they were grateful. Gene only voiced his disapproval once. I had let slip that I was a total Judy Garland fanatic and he'd recorded 'Over The Rainbow'. I said, 'No disrespect to you but I think that's a song that can only be sung by one person.' He wouldn't hear of it. He said he was doing it differently and I should appreciate his interpretation."

Marty Wilde: "If you got Gene singing ballads in the dressing-room, he would never stop. He sang ballads like 'Over The Rainbow' beautifully, really lovely."

The first date of the Gene Vincent and Eddie Cochran tour was at the Granada, Ipswich on Sunday 24 January 1960. In a feature for 'Hit Parade', Gene spoke of his love for Mantovani – "His great orchestral sound never fails to knock me out." He referred to working harder than he had ever worked. That was the best way for Gene to be – if he wasn't working, he was brooding. When a reporter asked Eddie Cochran what he was looking forward to, he said, 'Sleep.'

EMPIRE
LIVERPOOL

LARRY PARNES

presents

MONDAY, MARCH 14th

ONE WEEK ONLY

A Fast Moving Beat Show

1 OVERTURE ... ... The Hippodrome Orchestra

2 BILLY RAYMOND *Your host and compere*

3 TONY SHERIDAN TRIO ... *From TV's "Oh Boy"*

4 JOE BROWN ... *From TV's "Boy Meets Girl"*

5 BILLY RAYMOND introduces

For the first time in England
EDDIE COCHRAN
*Hit Recorder of "C'mon Everybody"
and "Summertime Blues"*

INTERMISSION
THE EMPIRE ORCHESTRA

6 GEORGIE FAME ... *New Singing-Pianist*

7 BILLY FURY ... *Britain's Newest Teenage Idol*

8 BILLY RAYMOND ... *Star of H.M.V. Records*

9 The Rock 'n' Roll Idol of Millions

GENE VINCENT

Backed
(by kind

FULLY LICEN

Tony
Sheridan

JOE BROWN
The Darktown Strutters' Ball;
Swagger

(Decca F11207)★★★

JOE BROWN (from "Boy Meets
Girls") accompanied by a group
he calls The Bruvvers. Revival of **The
Darktown Strutters' Ball** is fairly
straightforward with Joe singing and
playing guitar. Could branch out from
the juke boxes, and much depends on
just how many fans Mr. Brown has
acquired of late.

Swagger has the sound effect of
walking feet to underline the title. No
vocal from Joe this time, but a line of
comment is thrown in for a laugh. Side
is a useful instrumental with Brown's
guitar leading the section.

BILLY RAYMOND
" Seven Daughters "
" One In Particular "
(H.M.V. POP 526)

GEOFF LOVE has scored
some excellent Latin
sounds to introduce "Seven
Daughters" while the Rita
Williams Singers provide the
"lah-dee-dahs". I may be wrong,
but I have the feeling in listening to the side that Billy would
improve considerably if he
learned to relax. Though his
performance is competent, it
could be better.

"One In Particular" opens with
marvellous big band sounds from
the boys who work for Love.
And all the way through Geoff
has come up with fine ideas,
including some nice choral work
in the middle part. It's a cute
song, well recorded and
arranged.

BILLY
FURY
THAT'S LOVE

45-F 11237 Decca

Eddie Cochran

HALLELUJAH, I LOVE HER SO

[HLW 9022]

EDDIE COCHRAN
Hallelujah, I Love Her So; Little
Angel

(London HLW9022)***

WITH a thump and a wump and a guitar mingling with strings, Eddie Cochran whoops up a good ~orm as he sings, Hallelujah, I Love ~er So.

An infectious offering that may shape as a heavy seller for Eddie. If it does make the charts he ought to say a very big thank you to the arranger and musical director, who are, unfortunately, not named on the label.

Little Angel reverts to slow beat with a chorus repeating the phrases.

TEDDY JOHNSON'S Music Shop

PEARL and I gave our prophecies for 1960 last week. We now see that this age-old gambit has been practised by certain American critics.

They state that 21-year-old Eddie Cochran will be "The Singing Sensation of the Sixties."

He is following the time-honoured pattern of pop singers—after a hit disc he is being considered for the long-term contract deal with 20th Century films that is the crock of gold at the end of the vocal rainbow.

He is due to be seen on colleague Jack Good's show "Boy Meets Girls" on January 16 and 23, when it is highly probable that he will sing "Hallelujah, I Love Her So."

EDDIE COCHRAN—"The singing sensation of the sixties"?

Eddie Cochran film deal?

EDDIE COCHRAN, due here early next week for appearances on "Boy Meets Girls," may sign a long-term film contract with Twentieth Century Fox.

Cochran's British visit will last for ten weeks, during which time he will embark on an extensive tour of one-nighters with Gene Vincent. This opens at the Gaumont, Ipswich, on January 24.

EDDIE COCHRAN'S TOUR HERE — TEN WEEKS

AN exciting teaming of two of America's leading young rock stars has been achieved—with the arrival in Britain next week of Eddie Cochran, who is scheduled to remain here for ten weeks.

Cochran co-stars with another U.S. beat singer, Gene Vincent, in Larry Parnes' extensive promotion of one-night stands—commencing January 24, at Ipswich Gaumont. The tour also showcases British singer Vince Eager.

Dates following the Ipswich opening are Coventry (January 28), Worcester (29th), Bradford (30th), Sheffield (February 7), Taunton (14th) and Cardiff (26th)—all Gaumont theatres. There are thirteen other bookings awaiting confirmation for next month.

The package will probably play five-weeks in variety after the stint of one-nighters.

A summer matinee season now being negotiated would star Gene and possibly Vince at the Queens, Blackpool, opening about July 23.

Cochran and Vincent share the same manager, Norm Riley, who is expected to make the trip with Eddie: their arrival is scheduled next Saturday (January 9).

Eddie's appearance to guest in AR-TV's "Boy Meets Girls" on January 16 and 23 are now confirmed. His latest disc, "Hallelujah, I Love Him So," is released by London today (Friday).

COCHRAN, VINCENT CO-STAR IN TWO 'BOY MEETS GIRLS'

TWO of America's leading exponents of rock 'n' roll, Eddie Cochran and Gene Vincent, are showcased in the same television programme — when they co-star in ABC-TV's "Boy Meets Girls" presentation on February 20 and 27.

The two beat singers begin their joint nation-wide tour of one-nighters this weekend, and this will be interrupted to allow them to play these TV shows.

The February 27 programme (to be telerecorded on the 19th) will also include American singer David Winter, who was in the Broadway cast of "West Side Story" until recently.

Other bookings include the return of Davy Jones (January 30) and new Columbia singer Peter Wynne (February 20).

Producer Jack Good will shortly start preparing a new-styled programme for ABC-TV, scheduled to commence seven weeks after the last "Boy Meets Girls" show.

Said Good: "I assume that this new show will start on April 23, after Ernest Maxin's programme has run six weeks. I have not yet thought of a new format."

72

6. FROM HIPSWICH TO THE GRAVEYARD
Start of Gene and Eddie tour

"Two of us riding nowhere…
Two of us sending postcards…
Two of us wearing raincoats…"
('Two Of Us', Beatles)

One of the most telling photographs from the rock'n'roll era is of Brian Bennett on a train station, carrying his drum-kit. There's no doubt that this guy has paid his dues. He had just got married and he was out on the road. "That's me on Bexhill station on the Eddie Cochran tour. We were paid £20 a week and we had no transport and we went by train a lot of the time. I was on British Rail carrying five or six drum cases as there were no roadies. It was like that and we didn't moan about it. We just accepted it. Very often there weren't through trains from one destination to another, and if you are going across the country, it was particularly bad. I don't know how many changes there would be to go from Bristol to Newcastle, but it would have been a lot."

And that's not all. "When the shows were over, I had to think about my drum-kit. What should I do with it? Sometimes I left it at the stage door, providing I could be sure that someone would be there in the morning when I'd want to collect it: sometimes I took the drums to the left luggage department at the train station, and sometimes I took them back to the digs."

Larry Parnes needed a double top because he wanted to move away from one-nighters. If the touring package was to remain at a large theatre for a week, he needed a strong bill to attract the audience. A twice nightly tour of one night stands might attract 4,000 customers, but a week in one place meant 25,000 patrons. Fans hadn't acquired the habit of following a band around the country so all 25,000 had to come from the catchment area. Hence, he devised two different supporting bills for Gene and Eddie. Although the artists shimmied around because of other commitments, Parnes effectively had two packages. Gene and Eddie with Vince Eager and some lesser lights for the one night stands and Gene and Eddie with Billy Fury and Joe Brown for the weekly stints. To help them on their way, both 'Wild Cat' (Vincent) and 'Hallelujah I Love Her So' (Cochran) were in the Top 30.

There was a warm-up date with two houses at the Gaumont Theatre in Ipswich on Sunday 24 January 1960. Vince Eager had been working up north and hadn't met Eddie until that evening. Eddie was going on before Vince Eager in the first half. Eddie wore a silver waistcoat with black leather trousers. His first words to the audience were "It's great to be here in Hipswich" and then gyrated his hips, thus getting screams from the female fans. He received tremendous applause and had to do an encore. When interviewed by a local reporter, Eddie commented, "I was surprised to see older people here tonight" to which the reporter replied, "They're not all squares, the older ones."

Vince Eager: "When the curtains drew back, Eddie had his back to the audience and he opened with 'What'd I Say'. He knocked me for six. He looked great and he sounded great. As soon as he came off, I had to get ready to go on and I thought, 'What am I going to do here?' I had been doing 'Somethin' Else' as my opening number but I had to drop that."

Wally Whyton: "Eddie was dynamic. Nobody could hold a candle to him. He was absolutely tremendous, good-looking and young. He had things that our kids didn't have here. The Americans seemed to have this glowing, positive way of doing things and Eddie Cochran, he was swagger, man, he was cool, he was it. He was a tremendous performer."

Vince's big number was Conway Twitty's ballad, 'It's Only Make Believe'. "It was always a good number for me because I could milk it and, unknown to me, Eddie was at the side of the stage watching my set. The Gaumont in Ipswich was a lovely old theatre with lots of dressing rooms so we didn't have to share. I'd only been in my dressing room a couple of minutes when Eddie knocked and came in. He said, 'I really enjoyed your set, man. That's the best version of 'It's Only Make Believe' that I've ever heard.' Anytime you want to, come over to my dressing room. So I did. I'd often sit with Eddie and we hit it off great." In an interview a couple of weeks later, Eddie was asked for his best friend in the business and he responded not with Gene Vincent, but Vince Eager.

The first night of the tour worked well, especially as they had had few rehearsals. But there was a portent. The stress of being away from America and the pain in his leg was getting to Gene. He flew into a temper and shouted abuse at everybody and worse. Hal Carter: "Gene used to carry a gun and a knife around with him and he had a street gang mentality. One night he terrorised the bus as we were coming back from Ipswich. He ripped the bass player's brand new suit with his flick-knife, which he called Henry. He threatened about five of us. We all lived in North London but as soon as we got to the lights in Romford, the driver opened the door and we piled out and got a taxi home." (I suspect that it was Carter's suit that was ripped, but he didn't want to admit it.)

For the next two days, there were rehearsals at Max Rivers' Club in Gerrard Street, Soho. Eddie had seen the band in action and they were good: now he had two days to really knock them into shape.

Joe Brown: "Eddie had a great trick, it had probably been used in America for years, but we didn't know about it over here. He used to put a second string instead of a third string on his guitar, so that he had an unwound string and he could bend it and get those bluesy sounds that you never heard in England. That was the greatest thing I learnt from Eddie and as a result, I got loads and loads of session work with Adam Faith and others."

Johnny Gentle: "Joe Brown's eyes used to light up when Eddie played the guitar which was proof that he had something. He had this way of plucking the bass strings while playing the treble. You didn't really need a bass guitarist on stage because he was doing it with his thumb. I suppose he had got it from Chet Atkins but this was rock'n'roll rather than country."

Marty Wilde: "As I had no work for the Wildcats at the time, Larry Parnes had suggested that Eddie used my band. I didn't mind at all and when I told them, they were delighted. Eddie was Big Jim Sullivan's idol and it really showed in his playing - just listen to 'Trambone' by the Krewkats. Eddie had a fabulous stage act - he was a raunchy, loose-limbed guy who came out and enjoyed himself. There was nothing pretentious about him. He was an extremely good musician and he was ahead of most people musically and I don't think he would have stayed with rock'n"roll. You'd have heard a lot more of him in the 60s." Georgie Fame says something similar: "He might have got into country rock. I could see him doing stuff like Tony Joe White." Brian 'Licorice' Locking: "Eddie revolutionised our playing completely. We met in the basement at 44 Gerrard Street and we played 'Summertime Blues' first and we were rubbish really. Eddie said very nicely that we should do it this way or that. He was totally in charge and he knew what he wanted. He was the pivot that swung things around for us."

Brian Bennett, drummer with the Wildcats: "Eddie was terrific, right in the Presley mould, and he taught me a lot about playing rock'n'roll 'cause he played drums, bass and guitar. A lot of rock'n'roll rhythm was very simple and he was interested in changing bass-drums patterns and doing very different things with the bass drums. He used to give me very precise instructions about the drum fills he wanted. I'd come out of the dance band era and I was used to four to the bar or the bass drum on the first and third beats. Eddie taught me to develop independence between my feet and my hands and I'm still grateful to him for that. I used to work out a syncopated pattern with the bass player for 'Sweet Little Sixteen'."

In terms of professionalism, the three Viscounts had a clever 15 minute act. Gordon Mills, Don Paul and Ronnie Wells had been part of the Morton Fraser Harmonica Gang and they became a vocal trio with comedy and impressions. They developed a routine based around the revolving stage at the end of 'Sunday Night At The London Palladium' and they impersonated the Mudlarks, the Vernons Girls and the operatic David Whitfield. Their performances held them in good stead and they had hits with 'Shortnin' Bread' (October 1960) and 'Who Put The Bomp' (September 1961). Gordon Mills went into management with Tom Jones and Engelbert Humperdinck as his clients, while Don Paul produced Don Partridge and Paul and Barry Ryan.

Billy Raymond had studied music and drama in Scotland. He went up to London when he was 19 and his first job was the compère in a strip club, a thankless task if ever there was one. He sang on the BBC-TV show, 'You And The Night And The Music', and he recorded for HMV. His first single was a cover of Floyd Robinson's 'Makin' Love' in October 1959. The follow-up was 'Seven Daughters', but he chose to perform contemporary hits on tour: 'Only Sixteen' (he shared a flat with Craig Douglas), 'Living Doll' and 'Dream Lover'. He included impersonations of Johnnie Ray and Frankie Laine. He worked for Hymie Zahl's agency and it was Zahl who recommended him to Parnes.

Lance Fortune: "It depends on the audience but compères on beat shows often found it impossible to tell gags. They would end up spelling the names of the star performers, letter by letter, and the girls would scream at every letter. Billy Raymond was quite happy doing that. Anybody would be. It's easy money!"

After a day off for the performers on Wednesday, the tour continued on Thursday with a show at the Gaumont, Coventry and this time Eddie was closing the first half. The local paper said, "About 450 people, mostly young girls, attended the first half and screamed fairly steadily throughout the show, not, one felt from hysteria, but rather because it was the done thing." The second house drew 2,500 and the reviewer acknowledged that Gene excelled with 'Summertime'. The reviewer said, "The most interesting feature of the evening was the audience fashion display. One young man took the eye with his elegant ensemble of fur-collared coat, cravat, suede shoes and umbrella." Cutting-edge trends in Coventry then.

Eddie Cochran met a local reporter, Ron Scobling, backstage and was genuinely interested in others and what they did. Ron's friend, Alan, followed Manchester United and Eddie wanted to know more about soccer.

On Friday, they entertained the crowds at the Gaumont, Worcester, and stayed nearby at the Star Hotel in nearby Foregate Street. Buddy Holly had appeared there in March 1958 when a brick for whatever reason had been thrown through the dressing-room window. One fan, Trevor Booth recalled, "Eddie came on stage wearing a red shirt and a silver waistcoat, carrying a big Gretsch guitar and a little amp. He plugged it in and went 'Bang' straight into 'Somethin' Else'. The whole place went mad as he was so vibrant and exciting."

The show was 'a great success' according to the 'Worcester Evening News And Times' and Gene said that he was performing 'Over The Rainbow' "to prove that a rock'n'roller can really sing properly if he wants to." The reviewer added, "Whether or not, he proved his point is a matter of personal opinion." That's a no from him then. He concluded, "Billy Raymond put over a comedy act when all that the crowd wanted was more rhythm, but still he managed very well."

The coaches were from Timpsons of Catford: how's that for a bit of gratuitous research? Gene sometimes sat at the front of the bus, whittling a piece of wood away with his knife, which could make the others nervous, especially when he had that glazed look on his face. Sometimes too he took his gun out and blew down the barrel.

Vince Eager had a Vauxhall Vanguard and he sometimes took Gene and Eddie with him to the next gig. Gene liked the car as it had a seat in which he could sit comfortably with his bad leg. Gene did, however, hate being driven in the UK. He always thought he was on the wrong side of the road. Vince Eager: "Gene had terrible problems with his leg and I wasn't really aware of how bad it was until we played Worcester. The hotel we stayed in was very close to the theatre and Gene was in agony that night. Eddie and I went to his room because Gene was having trouble just walking, and when we got there, he took off his leg-iron. I'd never seen anything like it. His leg was one hell of a mess." It meant that Gene was on an immensely short tether and anything might set him off: remember too that theatres were not catering to the disabled, especially back stage.

It was snowing when they went to the Gaumont, Bradford, which could seat 3,000, and there were the first public signs that the tour might not always go smoothly. The 'Yorkshire Post' reported, "More than 2,000 teenagers at a rock'n'roll concert at the Gaumont, Bradford on Saturday night were astonished when the American star of the show, Gene Vincent, stopped in the middle of a song and walked off stage. His accompanying group faltered to a ragged halt, and harassed compère Billy Raymond hurried from the wings to the microphone to lead a finale in which all members of the company including a solemn-faced Vincent took part." It is possibly the only show Gene Vincent ever gave in which he never sang 'Be-Bop-A-Lula'.

So what had gone wrong? The brave reporter sought out Gene Vincent, 'a former seaman', after the show. "Four guys at the back had been heckling throughout the act," he said, "I didn't particularly mind during my fast numbers, but when they tried to ruin 'Over The Rainbow', I just couldn't take it any more. It is one of the best things I do and it has been going down well all over the country. I will never play at this place again." It would seem that the hecklers were not interested in finding out if "a rock'n'roller can really sing properly if he wants to." They shouted at him to return to rock'n'roll and the call to bring back Eddie Cochran did it for Gene.

Mike Priestley of the 'Telegraph And Argus' recalled that Eddie smiled teasingly at the audience after every song and "took his comb from his pocket and ran it through his quiff. He was so cool on that cold Bradford day." Not, however, after the show where both Gene and Eddie decided not to talk to fans.

As if to notify north-west hecklers, the journalist George Harrison drummed up publicity for their appearance at the Liverpool Empire in March. He told 'Liverpool Echo' readers that Vincent was barracked with calls of "Where's your motor-bike?" in Bradford and that the heckling reached such a pitch that he left the stage.

On Sunday, it was two shows at the Guildhall, Southampton at the unusual times of 3pm and 8.15pm, and this time the California boy, Eddie Cochran was struggling with the British winter and had laryngitis. He still performed but apologised during his set. The reviewer from the 'Southern Evening Echo' said that the all-black Vincent was attired "as though equipped for a deep sea dive or an inspection of the corporation dump". Vince Eager is said to be "a pleasant personality perched on quivering legs", but the reviewer's assessment of the best voice of the night belonged to Billy Raymond. "A pity he only sang a couple of numbers." What was the overall view? "It became progressively monotonous as it went on, song after song being shaped in the same old tiresome mould. So to the end and out in the cool, cool evening air; out into the pleasant melody of screeching brakes, klaxons and fearsome motor exhausts."

An annotated programme has come to light which shows the songs performed one night on the tour:

Tony Sheridan Group: 'Just A Little Too Much', 'Great Balls Of Fire'
Viscounts: 'Tallahassee Lassie', 'Rockin' Little Angel', 'Teenage Hop'
Eddie Cochran: 'What'd I Say', 'Somethin' Else', 'School Day', 'Sweet Little Sixteen', 'Hallelujah, I Love Her So', 'C'mon Everybody', 'Twenty Flight Rock'
Vince Eager: 'Yes Tonight Josephine', 'San Miguel', 'Why', 'It's Been Nice', 'It's Only Make Believe', 'What Do You Want To Make Those Eyes At Me For', 'Please Don't Touch', 'Puttin' On The Style'
Billy Raymond; 'Dream Lover', 'Livin' Doll'
Lance Fortune; 'Whole Lotta Shakin' Goin' On', 'My Babe'
Gene Vincent: 'Baby Blue', 'Over The Rainbow', 'Rocky Road Blues', 'Wild Cat', 'Be Bop a Lula', 'Say Mama', 'Summertime', 'Frankie And Johnny'.

The first full week of the tour at one venue was at the Empire in Sauchiehall Street, Glasgow from Monday 1 February 1960, twice nightly and so it was a total of 12 shows. The theatre filled touring variety companies with dread as the audience was remarkably cruel with comedians from south of the border. Bottles would be hurled at comics that they particularly disliked. Fortunately, the comedian was Scottish and as this was "A Fast-Moving Anglo-American Beat Show" with a much younger audience, things should have been all right. Eddie, indeed, was very sympathetic towards Billy Raymond and admired him for coping with hecklers.

The light operatic singer, John Hanson, remembers, "It was always the same for English comics at the Glasgow Empire. There would be a deathly silence followed by a slow handclap. It was quite horrendous and it frightened you if you were backstage and waiting to go on. Fortunately, they were kinder towards singers and I had glorious audiences when I was in 'The Student Prince'."

The tour now included Billy Fury and Sally Kelly, while the singer/pianist Georgie Fame was allowed to open the second half. Georgie Fame: "It was fantastic. They were gods. It was a marvellous experience working with the British musicians who were backing them like Big Jim Sullivan on guitar and Brian Bennett on drums. I used to stand in the wings and watch everyone working and, if anybody was late for a cue, I would run on and dep. Larry Parnes eventually gave me my own spot, which is when he christened me 'Georgie Fame'. The programme for the Eddie Cochran-Gene Vincent says, 'Georgie Fame, the new singing pianist.'"

The only sound check for the singers would be at the start of the tour. The band would go for the sound checks elsewhere and they would put anybody up front to sing the songs. If it was okay for him, then it was okay for everyone. However, Eddie happened to be around for one of the sound checks in Glasgow. Brian Bennett: "Georgie Fame knew some jazz chords and he did love jazz. He couldn't believe that I knew Thelonius Monk's 'Round Midnight'. He thought of me as a rock'n'roller but I'd learnt my trade long before rock'n'roll came along. Eddie wasn't impressed when he saw us playing 'Round Midnight'. It wasn't his scene." A year later, Fame was sacked by Parnes for daring to play jazz in concert on a beat show.

Jim Sullivan: "We were young and we were all trying to learn as much as we could. We had books on jazz and classical music and we would be asking each other questions all the time."

Joe Brown: "The first time I saw Gene he was drunk in a corner with a Colt .45 in his hand. We did a lot of shows together and he had a piece in his act where he would swing his leg iron over my head. He was very accident-prone and he was breaking that leg all the time. It was in plaster up to his thigh. Once he swung it up in his usual way, but he caught me on the side of the head. It knocked me flat and squashed my guitar."

Brian Bennett: "Eddie used to cringe at Broadcasting House because there would be only one microphone for the drum-kit and a couple for the guitars. His vocal mike was suspended from a large hook which he thought was very funny. The songs were almost cut live: we'd play one title and then Brian Matthew would say, 'That was Eddie Cochran singing 'What Did I Say'' and we'd go into another number. We'd do six numbers for 'Saturday Club' and the band would pick up ten-and sixpence each and then leave."

Once the stage was set for the weekly show, that was it. The only changes would be minor such as moving Eddie's amp to the centre of the stage. Hal Carter would get to the theatre early on the Monday and go through the charts with the theatre staff as they would use both the theatre lighting and the house PA. The stage lighting was rudimentary – single spot for sad numbers, and the like.

Terry Dene; "The lighting used to be pretty good at the Moss Empires. The lighting man would ask you about your numbers and you would work out whether you wanted a red spot or a blue background. It wasn't sophisticated by today's standards but it was very effective."

Hal Carter would stay with the lighting man for the two Monday shows and then leave it to him for the rest of the week. Parnes himself rarely appeared on the tours but Carter had to ring him each day with a report of the previous night, and Parnes would order performers to drop songs if they had died a death. Maybe it's just as well that Parnes wasn't around as Gene Vincent never had a good word for any promoter, except he would rarely repeat it to their faces.

Gene Vincent didn't bother with sound checks. He damaged a lot of mikes and promoters got upset about it. He hated AKG mikes as he couldn't get them off the stand. He might even throw them to the floor in frustration.

Eddie Cochran was really amused by Hal Carter's Scouse accent. Hal couldn't say 'Buddy' like the Americans could and it would come out like 'Boodie'. Eddie would ask him to say 'Buddy Holly and the Crickets' and when he was go on stage, Hal would call, 'You ready, Boodie'

The Liverpool singer and songwriter, Billy Fury, had been making an impact on 'Oh Boy!' and 'Boy Meets Girls' and although he was shy, his blatantly sexual stage act was the most provocative in the UK. Undeterred by some criticism in Ireland, Billy decided that he would make love to the microphone stand every night. As if to emphasise his manliness, he would strategically place the cardboard centre of a toilet roll down the front of his trousers. A golden quiff, a gold or silver lamé suit, a voice to die for and a bog roll. Hearts would melt. He had had hits with 'Maybe Tomorrow' and 'Margo' and he was perceived as the Next Big Thing. He was far superior to many of the US stars of the day and both Eddie and Gene appreciated his talent. Although Billy Fury had heart defects, this was not a problem on this tour. A consultant had told him that he didn't want to see him for six months, which he took as a good sign.

The saxophonist Ray McVay remembers, "I told them all that Glasgow was a terrible place to play as being Scottish, I knew what it was like. I thought they'd be whistling and shouting 'Geroff"!' As it happened, Gene and Eddie went down very well, although Billy had a hard time. Billy didn't mind though: he liked winding people up. He wasn't very mature and he thought the more he threw himself around the better."

The sturdy Glaswegian lads had no truck with Billy Fury's sexual posturings. The girls loved it of course, which incensed them even more. Joe Brown: "Being a sex symbol could cause problems. Some bird takes along a Teddy boy with a lethal quiff to see Billy Fury. He might wait outside the stage door to get Billy. He had a terrible time at the Glasgow Empire. They were throwing whiskey bottles, anything they could find at Billy. I was backstage and I heard the bottles coming through the air. The guitarists left the stage and in the end there was just Billy and the drummer left." On another occasion, the Teds ripped the ashtrays from the back of the seats and hurled them at Billy.

Joe Brown: "While Billy was strutting his stuff, giving the chicks their big thrill for the night, the blokes were sitting there simmering and swearing and threatening to kill him. It made me glad that my act was rock'n'roll and not sex."

Another evening when a highly apprehensive Billy Fury was waiting in the wings to perform, cracking his fingers as usual, Eddie Cochran came up to him. He told Billy to have confidence and say, "I am the best performer in the world. I am the best performer in the world." Billy did as he was told and Eddie said, "No, you're not, I am."

Jack Good had worked out a stage routine for Billy Fury, but Billy was always nervous before he went on stage, understandably so if an ashtray might be flying his way. Hal Carter said that Billy's ritual could take up to two hours: "He would put on his make-up, stand up and mumble back and forth, sit down, straighten his hair, stand up and mumble again, sit down, put make-up on the back of his hands, stand up and mumble, sit down, put tissues round his neck and his wrists, put on his stage clothes with ten minutes to go, turn up his collar, take off the tissues and go on stage. The tissues were to avoid getting make up on the clothes but once he was on stage he would get make-up all over them and they'd have to go to the cleaners the next day." Billy had both gold and silver lamé suits and if they weren't back in time, Billy would wear black suit, shirt and shoes on stage and be equally effective.

Hal Carter: "Billy loved Eddie and looked up to him. Billy kept his distance from Gene which was the most sensible thing to do. Billy wasn't a coward: he just didn't want to get involved." Tony Crane of the Merseybeats, who knew Billy well, recalls, "Billy never talked much about other performers but I got the impression that he was frightened of Vincent. He never knew how to take him."

Darlene hired a nanny for the children so that she could come with him to Glasgow for the week, which is fairly strange behaviour but we'll let it pass. They did some shopping together and Gene bought some tartan and a tam o'shanter. Gene told 'Hit Parade' that he was "initiated into the Kennedy clan when I was in Scotland a few weeks ago. That was on account of my grandfather being Scottish. I was presented with the clan badge and a roll of tartan cloth. I'm having the cloth made up into a complete outfit – slacks, jacket and tam o'shanter. I'm hoping to wear it in my stage act as soon as it's ready."

The Gene Vincent biographies are poor when it comes to researching his family tree. This book is the same but I plead that I am only dealing with the first four months of 1960. If Gene is telling the truth, it is likely to be the grandfather on his mother's side as their name was Cooper. There are Cooper tartans but not Craddock ones. However, there is a Cochran(e) tartan.

While in Scotland, Gene added a song about Bonnie Prince Charlie to his repertoire, 'My Bonnie': it's feasible that Tony Sheridan heard Gene doing the song, added it to his own repertoire and then, in June 1961, recorded it with the Beatles.

On the first show, Eddie Cochran talked about being in England and was heckled with cries of "You're in Scotland!" He was, however, also taken with Scottish customs and he went with their road manager, Hal Carter to buy some souvenirs while Gene was taking a bath and Darlene wasn't around. Before he left, he took Gene's leg iron and put it out of sight on top of the wardrobe. Eddie bought some sweaters as presents in Scotland. When they returned two hours later, they found Gene screaming at the hotel manager. He accused the hotel staff of stealing his leg iron and said that he would sue them for $1m. Eddie retrieved it from the top of the wardrobe and told Gene to calm down. The manager was furious with Cochran and almost threw him out.

Strangely, Gordon Irving, the NME's reviewer, found the rock'n'roll much too loud for him and considered the Viscounts to be the best on the bill. "It isn't a memorable beat show," said the reviewer, "but it does make an impact."

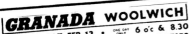

'Liquorice' Locking's photo of Brian Bennett on Bexhill Station carrying his drum kit

Vince Eager (Roy Taylor)

Left; Larry Parnes

LANCE FORTUNE

"THIS LOVE I HAVE FOR YOU"

Sally Kelly is another 'casualty'

SALLY KELLY, the young singer attached to Larry Parnes' "stable," entered St. Pancras Hospital on Sunday for an operation to remove a growth under her teeth. She is expected to be discharged at the end of this week.

As a result Sally Kelly's engagement at Finsbury Park Empire, on January 17, will probably be cancelled. She will appear as arranged, however, at the Granada, Greenford, on January 24, when she is billed with Marty Wilde.

Other dates Sally will be sharing with Marty are Sunday concerts at the Savoy, Northampton, on January 31, and the Lonsdale, Carlisle, on February 7.

Wildcats, Brian Locking, Eddie, Brian Bennett and Jim Sullivan

Peter Wynne

GENE VINCENT: PARIS THEN SECOND TOUR HERE

GENE VINCENT is to visit Paris in April. He will top the bill at the Alhambra Theatre while Eddie Cochran, his current co-star in Britain, goes to America for television and recording dates.

Vincent stars in the French capital for a week from April 17, then returns to begin a new ten-week tour with Cochran for Larry Parnes.

They open at Hanley Gaumont on April 30, and continue at Lewisham Gaumont (May 1), Cheltenham Gaumont (5th), Salisbury Gaumont (6th), Guildford Odeon (7th), Halifax Odeon (12th), Chester Gaumont (13th), Wolverhampton Gaumont (14th), Romford Odeon (15th).

In June and July, visits are scheduled to Rank theatres in Bournemouth, Plymouth, Weston-super-Mare, Southend, Colchester, St. Albans, Elephant and Castle (London), Sunderland, Derby, Edmonton, Kilburn, Folkestone, Southampton, Doncaster and Rochester.

U.S. rock stars for 'Saturday Club'

EDDIE COCHRAN and Gene Vincent, the American rock singer currently teamed on a nation-wide tour of Britain, are the star guests in BBC Light Programme's "Saturday Club" on March 5—the date Brian Matthew returns as resident host.

Accompanying them on the show will be Marty Wilde's backing unit, The Wildcats.

Also in this programme are Edna Savage, The Kentones, The Ted Taylor Quartet, The Brook Brothers and The Mike McKenzie Quartet.

The previous week (February 27) Don Lang, in his last week as compere, introduces his Frantic Five, with Joan Small, Dick Jordan, Johnny Duncan and The Squadcats.

The Eric Delaney Band makes a return visit to the Club on February 20, when it is joined by Glen Mason, The Maple Leaf Four, The Trebletones, Red Price and The Bert Weedon Quartet.

Rough trip to Paris for Gene Vincent

GENE VINCENT arrived back in Britain from Germany last week. He had quite a wild time in Europe, apparently. During a visit to Paris, he was mobbed in the streets, and the beautiful black suede jacket which he bought in Britain especially for his "Boy Meets Girls" appearances was torn from his back. Likewise his shirt. He was rescued from the crowd at last by the police, who escorted him to the theatre where he was appearing. He had to borrow somebody's jacket for his act.

On his second evening back in Britain, he went to the ballet—with Wee Willie Harris. Don't ask me how or why. I can't imagine. But I have it on excellent authority. What a picture! Vincent and Harris sedately mounting the steps of the Royal Opera House Covent Garden, dress in top hats, white ties and tails.

Good to see Gene has made the hit parade, by the way—he's been absent from it too long. The latest news is that he is to make his next single here in Britain! Well, well. Who's going to replace the Blue Caps, eh? My information is that a song written by Billy Fury is being considered.

"Boy Meets Girls" will be featuring Gene again on February 12.

GENE VINCENT (right) and Cliff Richard relax at "B.M.G." rehearsals—this was before his black suede jacket was ripped from his back.

7. "THEY GOT MY PANTS"
February 1960

"When I get to the top,
I'm too tired to rock."
('Twenty Flight Rock', Eddie Cochran)

The touring party became Gene and Eddie, Tony Sheridan, Vince Eager, the Viscounts and Billy Raymond for a series of one-nighters. The tour continued at the Gaumont in Sheffield. The reporter from the 'Sheffield Star' was unimpressed with Gene's 'hip swinging acrobatics', while Eddie Cochran's "harsh singing voice and jogging movements were a little wearing to both the ear and eye." On the other hand, "Vince Eager gave a first class performance and held his own with the more famous American stars."

This time Eddie was opening with "Somethin' Else", again with his back to the audience and wearing fawn leather trousers and a waistcoat. When he turned round with the spotlights turned on him, he was wearing dark sunglasses and again this looked really cool for Sheffield in February. His brooding "Milk Cow Blues" was one of several highlights.

John Firminger: "The Anglo-American Beat Show, as it was called, played in my home town at the Gaumont Cinema in Sheffield. This was truly an event and it was electrifying rock'n'roll. In the audience that night were many local up-and-coming musicians including Dave Berry, Jimmy Crawford, Frank White, Joe Cocker and Frank Miles. Both Dave Berry and Jimmy Crawford were taken with Gene Vincent and would be following in his footsteps, donning full leather gear as well as adopting his prowling stage movements. Frank Miles was lead guitarist with Dave Berry's Cruisers and was so impressed with Eddie as a musician and showman that he ordered one of the first Gretsch guitars to be used by a British musician." Gene, Eddie and Vince attended a special party organised by the Sheffield Star's Teenage Club in the theatre's Green Room Restaurant. Gene was pictured with the local band, Dave Berry and the Cruisers. They were interviewed by Teenage Club reporter, Carol Commander (née Ward), who helped to promote some UK appearances by Eddie's nephew, Bobby, in 1998.

Dave Berry: "I had previously seen Buddy Holly and was quite disappointed as he looked a bit like a dance band leader and there were only two Crickets. When I saw Gene and Eddie, it was like seeing real *proper* American rock-'n'roll for the first time. Both performers had a lot more edge and it was a revelation. They sounded great and looked great; Eddie moved around with plenty of confidence with the guitar whilst Gene crouched over the microphone, and both delivered the goods. These images stayed with me and I learnt from them. They certainly contributed towards my own stage presentation."

With snow and ice around, it wasn't the ideal time to be moving up and down the country playing a different venue every night. Vincent biographer, Rob Finnis: "Eddie was very homesick. He had come from California and the weather was a real culture shock for him. Gene didn't care much one way or the other - Bradford, Berlin, Hollywood, it was all the same to him." On 13 February 1960, they played the Granada Theatre in Powis Street, Woolwich. It had been called "the most romantic theatre ever built", but times had changed and it was mostly used as a cinema. The concert was pre-viewed by the 'Woolwich Kentish Independent', which described it as "a one-night stand by stars of the disco world". This is a surprisingly early use of the word 'disco'. Indeed, the Oxford University Dictionary cites 'Playboy' for the earliest use of the word in 1964.

Being close to military barracks, a number of servicemen went AWOL to attend the gig. Eddie explained his dark glasses by saying he had eyestrain – so he wasn't being cool after all – and he apologised for laryngitis. Many bikers and Teddy Boys were also at the concerts and Gene was on top form with a beautiful version of 'Over The Rainbow' and a slowed-down 'Be Bop A Lula'. The entire cast came on stage for a finale of 'What'd I Say'.

There was a Valentine's Day concert at the Gaumont in Taunton. Licorice Locking: "We were doing a one nighter in Taunton and I was joining the lads in Baker Street and we would travel down in a Volkswagen. I had made a phone call before we went and we were about halfway to Taunton when I realised that I had left my bag in the phone box. I had to go on stage that night in sports jacket and trousers. Someone found the bag too and I got it back."

The 'Somerset County Gazette' was dismissive of the show, criticising Gene Vincent for not speaking to the audience: "However, he did succeed in creating a mystery – what were the words to his songs?" Cochran was similarly discounted but the reviewer noted that "he had been suffering from laryngitis ever since his arrival in England. But despite this he was more comprehensible than Vincent was, and he was also more versatile." In con-clusion, the American stars were "little above the average standard of home grown products." The newspaper preferred Vince Eager (who closed the first half) and Billy Raymond and said that Cliff Richard received far more adulation at a recent concert. Considering that Tony Sheridan became such a wild performer in Hamburg, the comment on his performance revealed a quieter side: "Tony Sheridan opened the programme with restrained singing that was probably as good as any heard that evening but was too restrained to earn popular approval."

On 15 February, Gene made a live appearance on the BBC Light Programme's 'Parade Of The Pops' between 9.30 and 10.30pm and got 25 guineas. The host was Denny Piercy: Gene was backed by Bob Miller and the Millermen and the second guest was Maureen Evans. The next day,

Gene and Eddie went to Manchester to rehearse for 'Boy Meets Girls' for the two following Saturdays.

Jack Good produced Eddie for 'Boy Meets Girls': "I didn't change Eddie Cochran's act much because it was perfectly fine. My job was to sort out the camera angles to make him look his best. It's unfortunate that the 'Boy Meets Girls' shows were scrapped because they were so much better than the Dick Clark clips that you see nowadays. In America, they mimed to records and it was a wasteland. Gene and Eddie were delighted to be let loose as they both hated miming. We in Britain knew about show-biz, they knew about rock'n'roll, and so it was a perfect match. A couple of years later the Beatles combined show-biz with rock'n'roll perfectly, and the Americans loved it."

NME news editor, Derek Johnson: "I met them a couple of weeks before the crash. I thought Eddie was a very refreshing young man. He was full of star quality although he didn't try and act like one. He liked the short distances between venues because it was often a 1,000 miles or more in the States and he had avoided air travel since Buddy Holly's death. He told me his favourite of his own recordings was 'Sittin' In The Balcony' because it was his first gold record He planned to make an LP on which he would play all the instruments himself, which would have been years ahead of its time."

Hal Carter: "Eddie and Gene didn't bother with newspapers although they looked at 'Time' and 'Newsweek'. They read the music papers, particularly the NME, and Eddie also liked 'Punch'. They liked American comics and once, in Manchester, Eddie wanted me to get him some comics at midnight."

Considering Eddie's fondness for instrumentals, I wondered why Jack hadn't recorded any. "Have Eddie do some instrumentals? What on earth would be the point of that? He was quite short but he was so dynamic looking that I wouldn't have wanted to fill the screen with his guitar. He had a very strong visual sense of how to present himself. He was in control, he always knew how he should look to make an effect, and he would have made a wonderful actor. He was not your archetypal rock'n'roller, unlike Gene who just did things naturally."

Lyn Cornell from the Vernons Girls: "They were the same age as us but they were so much more experienced and had so much confidence. Eddie would joke with us a lot but we were so shy that we would just giggle."

Jack Good: "Eddie used to call me Watson and he knew of Sherlock Holmes through the Basil Rathbone films. He thought of himself as Holmes and me as the bumbling, British old colonel type. He gave me some grey leather gloves which he signed, 'To Watson, With love, Holmes'. Off stage, he wore very casual, American clothes. He was a sportsman and he told me that he was very fond of hunting, shooting and fishing. I thought he was going to be a hick because he came from Oklahoma, but he was a real gentleman."

Hal Carter: ""The only thing that got Eddie mad was if someone called him an Okie. He thought it meant he was thick."

Rob Finnis: "Eddie had the measure of Gene and I don't think even Vincent would have been stupid enough to have threatened Eddie. He knew that would have been the end for him as he depended so much on Eddie."

Hal Carter: "Eddie teased Gene. They had lots of mock fights, but sometimes Gene would get stroppy and Eddie would keep him in check."

Marty Wilde: "The black leather was Jack's idea but it suited him perfectly. He was a very rough character. He often pulled out knives, although he was always fine and polite with me. Eddie and Gene had a few fights, like two brothers. A few chairs were thrown around but they always ended up with their arms around each other's shoulders."

Jack Good: "Eddie and Gene didn't drink when I wanted them to work. I was too disciplined to allow that, but I did have long drinking sessions with them in Manchester."

Music writer Roger Dopson: "The amount of drinking that Cochran and Vincent did was beyond belief, particularly to the other musicians who were only starting to get used to pints of bitter."

Alan Holmes from Sounds Incorporated: "Gene wasn't very concerned about eating and he could never understand English hotels saying that dinner was served between noon and 1.30. He thought you should be able to take all the time you wanted over lunch. He also was irritated that we didn't have the American habit of having glasses of water at the table. He would say to the waiter, 'Sir, I will pay you for a glass of water and some ice.'"

Gene and Eddie used room service for late night food. For the other musicians, who were largely in digs, the meals might be at set times. Because of the time, Eddie might ring his mother for two hours after the show, an expensive business considering the cost of hotel calls. Despite this, Gene often shared a room with Eddie, really so he could give out the orders. Eddie's mother worried that he was eating badly. After all, he couldn't get hamburgers in Britain.

Jim Sullivan: "Coming to England was a big culture shock for them. The first time they were given fish and chips, it was in a great soggy mess, huge lumps of mush. They couldn't believe that we ate it. They did get to like it though." Bobby Rydell, also playing UK dates, declared, "It is the newspaper wrapping that gives them the flavour. I'll never eat off a plate again." If all else failed, he could be a restaurant critic.

Brian Bennett: "I don't think they thought about food too much. Whatever they ate was washed down with drink. They were the wildest characters that we'd ever come across. They used to disappear into the night. We didn't know where they went but in the mornings they were always very quiet."

Jim Sullivan: "The transport cafés were geared for truck drivers and it was all greens and gravy and puddings. Hamburgers were non-existent. I've seen Joe being very funny in the cafés as he would come out with Cockney rhyming slang. Eddie and Gene didn't always understand him but they loved to hear him talk."

A close friend from the later years Adrian Owlett states, "Billy liked cannabis which he first came across on the tug boats. Gene was not into dope at all, but Billy was very impressed when he saw Gene and Eddie at 'Boy Meets Girls' in Manchester sharing a pipe of Moroccan Gold. He'd only seen it in cigarettes before."

Don Paul of the Viscounts adds, "There was quite a bit of marijuana on those tour coaches but nothing else was around then."

They smoked all the time, Gene more than Eddie and preferring Capstan Full Strength. If Gene was given a cigarette with a filter, he would rip it off and say with some distaste, 'I don't smoke them.'

Although Gene Vincent would close the theatre shows, Billy Fury was more impressed with Eddie's dynamic performance. He and Jack Good had worked on his own act, but Eddie was his own man and knew exactly how to create an impact. Eddie was only a year older than Billy but he exuded experience and confidence.

On Thursday the tour was in Leicester for two houses at the De Montford Hall: best-seats only 7/6d. The reviewer from the 'Leicester Mercury' loathed the show: "I can appreciate a tune with a foot-tapping beat as much as anyone, but last night's exhibition of 'talent' sickened me. It was not so much the singing, because there was so much yelling going on I could hardly hear it, but the fact that these 'singers' seemed to get such enjoyment out of leg-kicking, face-pulling and making the youngsters scream. I cannot believe this is true entertainment. Then, why do these idiotic teenagers behave in such a ridiculous fashion? The way in which they shrieked, jumped up, and ran to the stage in a desperate effort to touch their idols was pathetic, as well as slightly disgusting. I can only hope that last night's audience were not typical of Leicester's young people."

After Leicester, Gene and Eddie returned to Manchester to work on 'Boy Meets Girls', staying at the El Morocco Hotel in Didsbury. They recorded two performances, one for the following day and one for February 27. The first show demonstrated that Eddie didn't mind cutting his songs down to 30 second soundbites. It was effectively a commercial for the tour and the programme ended with one of their finales, Willie Dixon's blues song, 'My Babe' with the addition of Marty Wilde and other cast members. The highlight of the show was a blistering performance of 'Milk Cow Blues': strong stuff for Saturday teatime. On the second show, Eddie gave a gruff-voiced performance of Teddy Randazzo's ballad, 'I Don't Like You No More', and recorded a duet of George Jones's country hit, 'White Lightnin'' with Gene Vincent.

The reason that they had to record that Saturday's 'Boy Meets Girls' was because they had two houses at the Caird Hall, Dundee. A local artist called Clyde Wells was added to the bill. Dundee was a trouble spot for touring rock'n'roll performers as Tommy Steele recalls, "We played a concert hall in Dundee, which held a few thousand people. In order to get some more money, they also sold the seats for the choir at the back of the stage. I told them it was a mistake and I was just sandwiched between all these fans and they came at me from both sides. I went into hospital and gave up touring after that."

Brian Bennett: "The Caird Hall and the De Montford Hall were dreadful places to play. They had long flat walls at the back and I'd hit the bass drum and it would echo back about two seconds later. With all the screaming going on, the musicians couldn't tell if they were hearing the drums or the echo."

There were 1,500 for the second house, which started at 8.45pm. Eddie created excitement by not having an introduction. The band played 'Summertime Blues' and Eddie came on, wearing a lumberjack's shirt and jeans. Two men (!) and a girl had fainted during Eddie Cochran's performance but generally, all was going well until 10.30pm, when six people were ejected from the hall and fighting followed. Three youths were charged with assault and a breach of the peace.

As Gene neared the end of his set, a girl came on the stage, threw her arms around his neck and kissed him. This was a cue for many more fans to invade the stage and Vincent was lost in the throng. The attendants moved them away and Eddie Cochran and Vince Eager came on for a closing number. This made things worse as an avalanche of screaming teenagers rushed the stage. The police arrived and they escorted the singers to the dressing rooms. Pandemonium followed in which seats and toilet fittings were damaged and, horror of horrors, the bust of the hall's benefactor, Sir James Caird, was pulled from its base and vandalised. Calm was restored by 11pm but by then the audience had started a sit-in and refused to move. Until the last buses, that is.

Hundreds waited in City Square for the artists to appear, but they hadn't realised that there was an alternative exit through a garage in a side street. Gene, Eddie and Vince, however, waited in a taxi until most of the crowd had gone. A group of fans tried to open their taxi at the traffic lights.

A city official said rock'n'roll concerts had created trouble in Dundee before, but this was the last straw and had to be the finish of rock'n'roll in the city. Dundee was now a rock'n'roll free zone. (Maybe still is: I've not been there for years.)

On consecutive days, Eddie and Gene went from Manchester to Dundee and then from Dundee to London, hardly a user friendly itinerary. Sunday 21 February 1960 was the date for the annual 'NME Poll Winners Concert' at the Empire Pool, Wembley. Gene and Eddie had not won any of the categories but they appeared as special guests. The bill, highly impressive for 1960 included Cliff Richard, Lonnie Donegan, Adam Faith and Billy Fury. As part of his new contract with Harold Fielding, Marty Wilde, reunited with the Wildcats, was given the closing spot. Things were going okay for Marty: his single, 'Bad Boy', was No.74 on the US 'Cash Box' chart and there were plans to go there in March.

Norm Riley and Darlene watched as Gene made the best of his 10 minutes by performing 'Say Mama' and 'Be-Bop-A-Lula' and at one stage he lay on his back, holding the microphone stand vertically above him. He had his quieter moments with 'Wild Cat' and 'Over The Rainbow'. Eddie pranced around the stage, performing 'Somethin' Else', 'Hallelujah I Love Her So', 'Sweet Little Sixteen' and 'C'mon Everybody'. According to the NME, "Eddie proved to be one of the most animated performers that America has sent us for a long time. Wearing black leather trousers, tartan shirt and silver waistcoat, he swung his guitar in a circular fashion across his body and pranced across the stage."

They remained in London for the next two days. On Monday 22 February, Eddie appeared on the Light Programme's 'Parade Of The Pops', backed by Bob Miller and the Millermen, and received 25 guineas for his trouble. The 'Radio Times' billing gives the guests as Eddie Cochrane (sic) and Craig Douglas. I don't know what Gene was doing that night but I can guess. Gene Vincent biographer, Rob Finnis: "Gene was always accusing people of sleeping with his wife, Darlene, but he was really goading them to see what would happen. She once said that Eddie was good-looking, so Gene beat her up. Another time, when he was drunk, he flung her out onto the street in Piccadilly. That's why she went home."

Henry Henroid: "Gene used to ring up Darlene and accuse her of being screwed by everyone. He had no idea of what was fantasy and what was reality. He explained it to me once by saying that he had witnessed his mother being screwed by a sailor and that he regarded her as a whore, but I've no idea whether he made that up as well."

On Tuesday 23 February, Eddie and Gene were at the BBC's Piccadilly studios in Haymarket during the evening to record for 'Saturday Club'. This was between 7 and 11pm and they recorded contributions for 5 March and 12 March. The host, Brian Matthew recalls, "We did a session at which they both appeared and we recorded Gene Vincent first. As he was leaving the studio, Eddie Cochran got on the tiny stage. He shouted, 'Hey, Vincent, you ain't going nowhere. I got your crutches. You're going to jam with me.' Gene went back and jammed with him for 10 or 15 minutes and it was great. Then he left and our engineer came out of the little control cubicle, which was on the balcony overlooking the theatre and he said, 'Was I supposed to be recording that?' We fell about because we imagined he would be thinking, 'Wow', and would be recording it."

Brian Matthew recorded interviews with the stars for 'Saturday Club'. Gene gives monosyllabic answers but Eddie was more forthcoming, saying that he played guitar, piano, bass and drums. He added, "I'll be here until April 17, then I go home for 10 days. Then I'm back near the end of April and I stay here for 10 more weeks." This was the first intimation that the tour was being extended.

Brian Bennett: "Gene would start a number with 'Welllll...' and we wouldn't know which number it was going to be. He was keeping us on edge rather like Buddy Rich. Buddy used to shout '48' or some other number to his band just before he started to play it. When we were playing, he used to turn around and look at me to egg me on. He was always pushing us along, agitating us, getting us to be more aggressive. He liked to stand right in front of my bass drum and he'd have us on edge with his energy."

Gene and Eddie were paid 25 guineas each for each programme and the musicians got £4 a man and porterage. An internal file memorandum shows that the BBC was having problems in complying with the Ministry of Labour's agreement with the Variety Artists Federation. "Foreign artists in the lesser known category" were restricted to only one radio or television appearance a month. As an artist would invariably prefer television, it was felt that this was unfair to radio producers. The category an artist fell into was determined by the size of the fee. Because Gene Vincent had been paid 25 guineas for 'Saturday Club', he fell into the lesser paid category and so the restriction applied. This was taken up with the Ministry of Labour and as an exception, he was allowed to make one radio *and* one television appearance a month. However, it is feasible that ABC's fee for 'Boy Meets Girls' put Gene (and then Eddie) into a better known category.

On Wednesday February 24, the tour resumed with two performances at the Globe Theatre in Stockton-on-Tees. They were not sell-out houses, but the audiences were again hysterical.

Eddie, like Gene, was bored by British TV. In the States, there was a TV in every dressing room. There was nothing here. He had a love of westerns and hardly saw any. When 'Valentine' asked him for his favourite British star, he singled out the middle of the road singer and comedian Dave King. The next day the touring party went to the Gaumount, Cardiff. Tony Sheridan had a torrid time as he was showered with lit cigarettes as the impatient audience wanted Gene and Eddie. The 'Cardiff And Suburban News' described Gene as "a leather-clad spaceman from another planet." About right there. The future rock'n'roll impresario, Paul Barrett, says, "Gene was wonderful, so good it makes his decline even harder to bear. Eddie was everything he promised to be in 'The Girl Can't Help It'. I have seen nothing better and I know I never will." While in Cardiff, Eddie recorded a hospital radio interview with Vic Dawe and after the show, both Gene and Eddie went to the Astor club with some local celebrities.

On Sunday 28 February 1960, Gene and Eddie travelled to Leeds and checked in at the up-market, Queen's Hotel in City Square, right by the railway station. They were playing a week at the Empire Theatre and this time it was the A-team with Billy Fury and Joe Brown as well.

When there were Sunday concerts, the Lord's Day Observance Society imposed strict rules and banned stage make-up, although the finer points differed from place to place. Larry Parnes: "There were Sunday laws in certain towns which had been created by the Lord's Day Observance Society. Sometimes you weren't allowed to wear stage clothes and make-up on a Sunday. I said in one place, 'Billy wears his gold lamé suit in the street so of course he can wear it on stage.'" The hapless Fury walked on the sea front to prove the point.

As usual, the reporter from the regional paper, this time the 'Yorkshire Post', was unimpressed: "The show is a prolonged assault on the eardrums, for despite the seven loud speakers on stage, the noise from that side of the footlights is more than matched by the screams of excited teenagers in every part of the theatre." The reviewer, clearly longing for the exit, added, "The youngsters anxious no doubt to show that they could take whatever was coming to them stuck it out." No, they were enjoying it, mate.

Whether you liked him or hated him, Gene Vincent always gave a reviewer something to write about: "Mr Vincent looks frankly macabre in a suit of black leather and gloves to match. Legs spread eagle, he sings almost throughout his performance from a crouching position, rarely facing the audience and occasionally shaking his head from side to side in a rhythmic frenzy."

And his favourite act: "Tucked away in the first half of the show is a youngster who, I feel has more than average talent beneath his rock'n'roll exterior. His name is Joe Brown. Raw and gawky at the moment, he could, with a little luck, make the grade as an all-round entertainer in the Tommy Steele manner."

Eddie wore black leather trousers, an orange shirt with the sleeves slightly rolled up and a silver waistcoat. He opened with his back to the audience and then went into 'What'd I Say'. He rolled his guitar across his hips for 'Summertime Blues' and it was followed by 'Somethin' Else' and 'Sweet Little Sixteen' and his familiar hits. A girl gave him a bunch of roses and he thanked her. Another gave him after shave and he said, "Smells pretty good to me, baby." Encouraged by the strong reception for Gene's 'Over The Rainbow', Eddie had worked out a sultry version of 'Fever' without his guitar and with just Licorice Locking on bass. Several girls fainted while he did this so St John's Ambulance Brigade was kept busy.

The Empire Theatre was on Briggate and Jimmy Savile managed the Mecca ballroom, which was just off Briggate. He invited Gene and Eddie to drop in if they wished. They came and in typical Savile fashion, he lectured the punters, "Look, Eddie Cochran and Gene Vincent are going to come over after they've finished their show. Politeness is the name of the game; if you give them any hassle, I'll turn them round and run them out. If you want to keep them, don't give them hassle and just say hello. Eddie and Gene walked in and it was like walking in to 1,000 friends. I took them to the snack bar area and they had tea and coffee and they had a superb evening."

But it wasn't always so. Hal Carter: "Eddie was drinking because he was homesick. He spent a fortune on the phone speaking to his mum. He'd be talking to her for an hour before the show and he was drinking Jack Daniel's like it was going out of fashion."

A few days later they were in Leeds and when Billy Fury found a girl hidden in the boot of his car, he took her to the cinema. According to press reports, Billy had 18 girlfriends in 18 months and presumably this was an extra.

After one show in Leeds, they travelled by car back to the hotel and Joe Brown recalled, "We stopped at the traffic lights. Gene was in the front passenger seat and Eddie and I were in the back. The door flew open and there were a lot of people jumping around and reaching into the car. The lights changed and the driver put his foot down and shot off. Everything was quiet and then all of a sudden, Gene said, 'Eddie, they got my pants.' They'd reached in, grabbed his leather trousers and got them off. He went into this posh hotel with no trousers and his leg iron exposed."

Eddie had been getting the girls but the last night in Leeds was a good one for Gene. Maybe too good…

IT'S EDDIE COCHRAN'S

turn to answer YOUR questions

put to him by KEITH GOODWIN

COSILY wrapped up in a fur-lined black leather jacket and leather trousers, American beat star Eddie Cochran turned away from the window looking out on a rain-swept Oxford Street and announced: "I don't like the weather, but everything else is fine. I couldn't be happier."

Eddie relaxed in an easy chair after completing rehearsals for his forthcoming concert tour, broke open a fresh packet of cigarettes, and declared he was "only too happy" to answer a series of questions I'd gleaned from readers' letters. His answers form this interview:—

? ?

Q. Who plays the guitar solos on your records?

A. I do! Always have done. I like playing guitar as much as singing. I'm self taught, and before I broke into singing I was a studio musician.

I played in all manner of accompanying bands in the Hollywood studios, such as the 20th Century-Fox, Warner Brothers and Capitol organisations.

? ?

Q. Is rock 'n' roll cooling off in America?

A. No, I don't think so. After all, rock is still pulling in the crowds all over the country. But rock has definitely quietened down. The beat's still there, but it's not as wild these days. It's more polished and seems to have matured. But it occurs to me that British fans still go for the wild stuff in a big way. The fans seem to be slightly younger, too.

? ?

Q. Have you ever sung in a vocal group?

A. Not in the strict sense. But I did sing bass on one of Gene Vincent's record dates for Capitol. He called up the night before the session, and asked if I'd like to handle the bass parts on an album he was doing. I thought it might be fun, so I went down to the studio the next morning and became one of the famous Blue Caps for a day!

? ?

Q. Have you ever recorded on bass, drums or piano?

A. Sure I have—on the "Summertime Blues" session, for example, I sang the solo voice, the bass voice that comes in now and again, and also wrote the song.

In addition, by multi-recording techniques, I also played guitar, bass and drums. I repeated the formula on another of my compositions, 'C'mon, Everybody'.

Then came "Somethin' Else," for which I wrote the melody, part of the lyric and also played bass and guitar. On my latest disc—"Hallelujah, I Love Her So"—I play piano, and I sit at the keyboard for quite a few of the tracks on my new album, which will be issued here soon.

? ?

Q. What sort of rôle do you have in your new film, "Johnny Melody"?

A. I appear in a guest singing spot in a night-club scene, and sing two of my own compositions — "Teenage Heaven" and "I Remember." But I'd like to get down to some serious acting when the right story and part come along.

I've done TV plays and I like acting. If I was offered a film part that I could get my teeth into, I'd certainly take drama lessons.

? ?

Q. Is your romance with screen actress Connie Stevens serious?

A. Well, we go out together a lot, and have seen each other for around six months. She's really a great girl—the sort of girl with whom it would be very easy to get serious. I can't really say anything more.

We haven't discussed marriage yet, but I'm a pretty impetuous sort of fellow, and diable to make a snap decision any time.

Q. What was the most significant lucky break of your career?

A. Appearing in the film, "The Girl Can't Help It." You see, I wasn't even a singer before I made the movie, and hadn't had any vocal discs at all.

How'd it happen? Well, one day I was playing guitar on a session when up comes a guy, and asks: "How would you like to make a picture?" I thought he was kidding, but said "Fine!" and asked him to call me.

Well, the next day he called and asked if I could sing. I went along with the gag, said I could, and then he asked me to make a demonstration disc of a tune called "Twenty Flight Rock."

I still thought it was a joke—let's face it, I didn't know if I could sing. Anyway, I made the record, he liked it, signed me for the film, and that was the start of everything!

Q. What was your biggest show business disappointment?

A. Hearing the playbacks after my first recording session. I cut "Sitting In The Balcony," and I didn't like it at all. But the disc went on to sell a million—and I was the most surprised of all. Even now, I still get a little disappointed hearing playbacks. I always feel I could have done better.

Q. What is the biggest drawback of being a star?

A. Not having time to be home with my friends, and having to go out with people I'm not really interested in. You see, back home I like to hang around with a gang of my old friends.

Q. Which do you prefer—films, TV or stage shows?

A. Give me stage shows every time. TV and films are fine, but I much prefer to work live. It's so much more exciting, and I feel I can get closer to the people. When an audience is enthusiastic, I get something from them and, in return, give a better performance. Audiences can be very stimulating.

But the publicity men don't like this. They get mad at me, and say I go out with the wrong people. But I like the company of my old buddies. It's all very confusing.

Q. Which, in your opinion, is most important—the melody, the lyrics or the singer?

A. A combination of all three is ideal, of course. But sometimes the melody is more infectious than the lyrics and vice-versa. It's also true that in many instances a singer can establish himself as a personality, and then the fans buy his discs just because they are his discs. That's when the singer becomes most important.

Q. Who has been the greatest influence on your career?

A. Without a doubt, Ray Charles. He's so good — one of the greatest blues singers I've ever heard. But I don't consciously try to copy him. I simply try to generate the same feeling that he produces when he sings.

Q. Do you carry any lucky charms on stage?

A. Well, I always wear a ring—I'd feel lost and ill at ease without it on stage. It was given me last October as a birthday gift by Jim Styvers—he's the piano player who leads my supporting band. We've been together quite some time, and the ring has great sentimental value.

Q. Can you offer any advice to aspiring singers?

A. First, you must find somebody to talk for you—a manager. That's very important, and I don't think you'll get too far without one. Next, I feel it's very necessary to be a perfectionist and to believe in what you're doing.

But I don't go along with the theory that a formal musical grounding is essential. Genuine enthusiasm and a certain "feel" for music is far more valuable in the long run.

Q. Who do you think is the most promising newcomer in America today?

A. That's a stiff question, but seeing as you've caught me on the hop, I'll settle for Brook Benton. He's real good—has style and polish. I'm surprised he hasn't caught on here yet.

Cochran—Vincent package hit extends tour to 20 weeks!

MANY OTHER U.S. STARS PLAN VISITS HERE

THE Eddie Cochran-Gene Vincent package tour has opened so favourably, that on Wednesday it was arranged that they continue in Britain for a further ten weeks—making 20 in all!

Cochran has two important television dates in America in April which had been arranged to follow his British tour. He will now fly to the U.S. for a fortnight for the TV shows and immediately return to London to resume with Vincent on April 30.

The pair opened to full houses at Ipswich on Sunday. Advance bookings for concert and variety dates are so good that their manager, Norm Riley, quickly arranged the extension.

He had planned to bring over another American star to join Vincent, but now intends to tour instead a completely new package to tour in September, leaving Eddie and Gene together until the summer.

The Cochran surprise came on top of news of another stream of activity for projected visits by leading U.S. stars.

Originally expected next month, Connie Francis is now due here early in May, cables Nat Hentoff. A five-week visit is planned, which must end by June 15 because of U.S. commitments.

A newcomer to Britain, expected late in March, is Brook Benton—one of the biggest-selling Mercury artists in America. Best known here for his Chart-entry "Endlessly," Benton's initial visit would be restricted to ATV appearances.

Negotiations are also proceeding for c-and-w personality Marty Robbins to make his British debut in the Spring—probably during May. It had been hoped to clinch a visit in the next few weeks to coincide with his current " El Paso " disc hit, but his heavy American commitments prevent this.

Among other top-selling U.S. disc-stars currently the subject of negotiations here are Frankie Avalon, Fabian and Conway Twitty.

Twitty is another likely May arrival. He would come for TV appearances and also a short tour. Both Avalon and Fabian are also scheduled for the Spring, or early Summer.

Pat Boone, who was set last week for a lightning visit in a fortnight to top ATV's " Sunday Night at the London Palladium," may postpone his trip—also until the Spring—when he would be able to extend his stay here.

GENE VINCENT (bottom left) is at present touring Britain, aiding the sales of his popular " Wild Cat " disc. EDDIE COCHRAN (bottom right), another visitor from America, appears on " Boy Meets Girls " this Saturday.

8. JACK DANIEL'S IF YOU PLEASE
Too much boogie, March 1960

"Jack Daniel's if you please,
Knock me to my knees"
(David Allan Coe single, 1979)

After the week in Leeds, Gene and Eddie were to take a train on the Sunday March 6 for their next week in Birmingham. Their train was delayed for over two hours. To avoid being pestered, they were put onto a stationary train. One fan was with them for most of the time…

Joe Brown: "They used to travel in the first-class compartment and we were stuffed in the cheap seats. Eddie used to tell someone to ask Joe to get his guitar. I'd go into their compartment but the ticket collectors would sometimes sling me back." Sometimes, too, Eddie and Gene would put the lights out in their compartment, pull down the blinds and sit there in the dark.

When the train eventually arrived in Birmingham, Hal Carter knew there would be trouble. Hal Carter: "I never liked Gene Vincent. From the moment I saw him, I thought he was a coward and a wimp. He used Eddie's friendship to get himself out of trouble. There were a lot of girls on the tour and there was one in particular that Eddie had met in Leeds. Gene had given her the money to get on the train from Leeds to Birmingham but when Eddie saw her, he asked me to 'get rid of that goddamned cow'. I gave her the money to go back to Leeds and she said, 'You do that and I'll call the police. I'm only 14.' Gene started whimpering and hollering, 'I told you, Eddie, not to bring that bitch'. He was blaming it on Eddie, which was absolutely typical of him." As usually happened, Eddie resolved the issue. He sweet-talked the girl saying, "I'm sorry, honey, but we've got to rehearse and we've got a show to do. You write to me and I promise I will write back. Okay?"

Eddie and Gene checked in at a hotel in the centre of Birmingham, while Billy and Hal were in Mrs Green's guest house. Hal told them that he would be back the following lunchtime as he wanted them at the sound check. When Hal got there, the hotel manager told him to get them out of the place. Gene and Eddie had held a party which turned into an orgy involving chambermaids and waitresses. The other hotels in the city were fully booked, so Hal moved them to Mrs Lovesey's guest house in Sparkhill, south-east of Birmingham. It was a theatrical boarding house and Joe Brown was staying there: Joe tended to find his own digs and he had friends all over the country. Joe would keep receipts of his travelling expenses and he asked Parnes to refund a taxi fare for 10 shillings. "But the fare is only nine shillings," said Parnes. "I had to give him a tip," said Joe. "A whole shilling!" Parnes exploded, "Threepence is quite enough."

The rooms in the guest house were small but, fortunately they liked Mrs

Lovesey and everything was okay. The main drawback was that they wouldn't have room service.

Joe Brown: "Vincent and Cochran were crackers, real crazy people, they were great. Gene was in a lot of pain with that leg of his. He used to drink so Eddie used to look after him and get him things and make sure he was okay. It was a funny relationship and I was always there in the middle of it all. Gene used to get a bit suicidal as well when we'd been drinking 'cause that leg was very painful. If it got really bad, Eddie used to put him to bed and while he was there, crooning to himself, Eddie and I would sit around playing our guitars and making sure that he wouldn't do anything silly. Ol' Vincent was a very sad case."

As usual, the regional newspapers sent their theatre reviewers to pass comment, mostly of a critical nature. They were at a loss to appreciate the music and 'The Birmingham Mail' concluded, "The Americans have some very nice leather trousers and Billy Fury wears gold lamé and violet velvet, which seems to please his fans." One reviewer thought that rock'n'roll was dying but "the young people proved that they have in no way lost their remarkable ability to drown out a performer's voice." He added, "It is difficult to take individual acts because from start to finish, there seemed nothing but nerve-shattering electric guitars and pounding drums."

Licorice Locking: "When we were at the Birmingham Hippodrome, they announced Gene Vincent and the drummer Red Reece wasn't there. The curtains opened and the band started playing so I just leapt on the drums and started playing. I had never played drums on stage before but it went okay and Eddie was watching me from the wings, very amused. Red came along after the first song and took over."

Two neighbours, Rita and Phil Peachey knew Mrs Lovesey and saw Joe Brown in the garden. He was having target practice with an air rifle and a dartboard. He invited them to come inside after the show and he would introduce them to Gene and Eddie. Still in his black leathers, Gene was worn out and Eddie said, "He's whacked, he's had it." During the week, Eddie closed the show for Gene, but this could have been because he was not feeling too well and wanted to finish early.

While this was happening in Birmingham, Marty Wilde was going about his career change. He had been featured on 'Desert Island Discs', which was broadcast on March 5, and his choice of records had included rock'n'roll, MOR standards and classical favourites. By the time of the broadcast, he was in America. He was featured on Dick Clark's 'American Bandstand' from Philadelphia and he and Joyce had a belated honeymoon on Norm Riley's ranch in West Covina, California. Before they returned to the UK on April 10, Marty recorded ten sides in New York including 'Little Girl', a UK Top 20 hit later in the year. Joyce was pregnant and Marty told the press that if it was a little girl, they would name her Kim.

On Sunday 13 March 1960, the touring party travelled to Liverpool. The shows were at the Empire Theatre on Lime Street and just a few hundred yards away, on the same street, was the Adelphi Hotel. The huge hotel was built at the turn of the century to give clients an idea of what staying on a liner would be like before they travelled to New York. The rooms were, and still are, like state rooms. The hotel is unique, still is, but for different reasons today as any reader of tripadvisor.com will tell you. It was the natural place for celebrities visiting Liverpool to stay. Bill Haley, Tommy Steele and Roy Rogers were there in the 50s and indeed, the local papers pretended that Trigger was a guest as well. He put his hoof print in the visitors' book but he was really staying in the police stables in Smithdown Road. Flanked by hundred of children, Roy Rogers rode Trigger down Lime Street to the Empire Theatre.

Jim Sullivan: "The Adelphi was like a big old, show-biz hotel but we couldn't afford the hotels. We would stay in boarding houses that were used to actors and actresses and music hall performers. We were with the cast from one of John Hanson's operettas, and these people never classed us as being in show-business. The dinner might be like a family gathering before the show and so that was quite homely, but the rooms would be something else again. They were very cold and we would have to put a shilling in the meter. I've also stayed in transport cafés to save money where it would be 10 shillings a night and 30 to a dormitory."

This time Eddie was closing the first half. The curtains opened in darkness and the intro of 'What'd I Say' played. The three guitarists turned round as one and there was Eddie, legs braced as the sound swept over him. He asked if there were any 16-year-olds in the theatre and dedicated 'Sweet Little Sixteen' to them. For the first time on the tour, Eddie sang 'Sittin' In The Balcony' and impressed the audience with his guitar-picking. A young John Peel was in the audience and he later remarked, "Eddie was great and Gene was even better."

Nik Cohn in his book, 'Awopbopaloobop Alopbamboom', says of Eddie, "He was a mover and a writer and voice. He played his own things on guitar, he was really a musician. He sang songs that weren't crap but did somehow manage to get across a real basic attitude. All of that was new. No poncing about, no dressing-up or one-shot gimmicking: he was something solid happening. So Billy Fury saw him and woke up. Or the Beatles saw him, or the Stones, or the Who, or the Move. That's how things got started." Paul McCartney was not at the Empire, but young George Harrison was most impressed with Eddie Cochran's guitar playing.

Well-known rock'n'roll writer, Jim Newcombe, was very impressed by what he saw on the Tuesday night, although Gene was wearing his bright green suit that night. He especially recalled Eddie shrugging his shoulders during 'Somethin' Else' and playing a chilling solo on 'Milk Cow Blues'.

The most savage of all the regional reviews of the tour was published in the 'Liverpool Daily Post' on 15 March. It was written by 'G.E', actually a staid, old-time reporter named George Elgin. He wrote, "The only man fitted to review this show at the Empire, Liverpool last night would be a psychiatrist. No one else could possibly understand or explain it. Larry Parnes, whose claim to fame is that he has discovered more teenage pop singers than anyone else, has conceived the idea of putting a whole flock of them into one show. Mr Parnes's claim is dubious because on the evidence of last night's effort any untalented kid who can clutch a microphone or guitar is a potential starlet."

Elgin, who had lost his marbles, comments on the complete absence of talent but he couldn't hear them above the screams. With one exception. "I did at one point, while one of the Americans, oddly attired in a black leather suit, was crawling about the stage clutching a microphone, catch a few phrases of a fearfully maltreated version of 'Over The Rainbow'. Apart from that, I have no idea what anyone was singing about."

The evening paper, 'Liverpool Echo', was similarly critical but, perhaps with a nod to 'G.E', said that nobody but teenagers had any place in the Empire that week. The singers "entrance the teenager audience and even get down to creeping about the floor and performing the strangest contortions."

Commenting on the local hero, Billy Fury in his silver lame suit, George Elgin wrote, "What will the boys on the tugs say about that?" Sam Hardie, the pianist with Kingsize Taylor and the Dominoes: "I remember seeing Billy Fury at the Liverpool Empire. I thought he was dreadful. He was caressing the microphone and I was very embarrassed about it. I suppose by booing him, I was showing off in front of my girlfriend, but a lot of others were booing him too."

Privately, Larry Parnes, on one of his occasional visits, was booing him too. "These are good clothes," he would argue, "and you are ruining them with your antics. If they have to be replaced, you will have to pay for them." Indeed, Billy was to wear the silver lamé jacket with black trousers once the original ones were beyond repair. Pete Townshend used to play his act with a decent guitar and then swap to a cheap one for the destruction. Maybe Billy should have done something similar.

Billy was treated as a star in Liverpool, especially when he returned home to the Dingle with a police escort. "He was as overwhelmed by his success as much as we were," says Billy Hatton. Billy brought home a pile of fan letters and asked his mother to answer them for him. This is rather better organised than Gene and Eddie who were happy to speak to fans at the theatres but rarely responded to letters.

Not all the shows were consistently good (or appalling, depending on who you are). Gene hated the rain in Liverpool and said that it affected his leg. He was in a bad, self-pitying mood for most of the week. Eddie who had had that hunting accident in his youth also had pains in his leg, which he attributed to the bad weather. He described his next single, 'Three Steps To Heaven' as a calypso so it was from calypso to collapso.

Billy Hatton, a childhood friend of Billy Fury's: "Billy got me backstage at the Liverpool Empire and I got to meet Eddie and Gene. Eddie saw me eyeing his guitar, his famous Gretsch, and he had two pick-ups on it, a Gretsch one and a Gibson. He asked me if I wanted to play it, and I was holding the guitar I had seen in 'The Girl Can't Help It'! There's me, Billy Hatton, playing Eddie Cochran's guitar. Billy Fury said to me, 'Put your hand out of the window' and all these girls screamed. I thought, 'I have got to get some of this.'" And he did. A few years later, Billy Hatton had hit records as part of the Fourmost.

There was no local radio then, apart from hospital radio. Monty Lister had been broadcasting to listeners at Clatterbridge and Cleaver hospitals on the Wirral from the 1950s and he would manage to get a few minutes in a dressing-room here and there, having Bill Haley, Marvin Rainwater, Freddie Bell, Lonnie Donegan, Cliff Richard and Tommy Steele among his many guests. Usually he did not set them up in advance and relied on friendly stage door keepers. His none-too-portable tape recorder weighed 35 pounds and had to be plugged into a light socket. He got Gene and Eddie to cooperate and I asked him how he found them. "Rather scruffy was my impression. They were lolling around and I had to chase after them with a microphone. They were both smoking and they weren't very tidy with their cigarette ends, but they were both very friendly."

Gene said that he would be in the UK until September and he promoted his latest record, 'My Heart', which was written by Johnny Burnette. Vincent did not care for the song but it had just entered the charts and every little bit helps. Commenting on 'Boy Meets Girls', Eddie said, "It is a very well produced show. It is superior to American rock'n'roll shows." He selected his current hit, 'Hallelujah I Love Her So', from his own records, and said that he was going home for 10 days on April 17 and then returning for 10 more weeks of touring.

The interviews sound quaint today but despite their brevity, Lister has captured the essence of their personalities: Cochran's eagerness, Vincent's disinterest, Brown's East End bonhomie and Fury's concern for hospital patients. While Monty is interviewing Billy Fury, you can hear the screams outside the window. Later in the week, Monty took two of the performers to meet factory workers in Port Sunlight and he recalls, "I took Billy Fury on a walking tour of Port Sunlight village and he asked me confidentially if he could buy one of the houses. They were tied cottages then so I said, 'Only if you work for Lever's'. He was a most likeable youngster, very shy and he wasn't fussy about talking on stage. He wasn't very happy with me when I introduced him with 'Gonna Type A Letter' which he thought was dreadful but I still like it. After we had done the lunchtime record programme, we went to the Bridge Inn, a posh hotel in Port Sunlight village for lunch and the service was dreadful. Joe Brown had a starting pistol on his person, as the police would say. We had had our soup and main course and we were waiting for the sweet. The Bridge Inn was like a cathedral, very quiet and very sober, but Joe fired his starting pistol in the air and people came crashing through doors from all around." An indication too that Joe was picking up on Gene Vincent's wayward behaviour.

Monty Lister had caught Gene and Eddie on a good day. When Gene said that he wanted a Coke, it usually meant Scotch. He would take both half-a-bottle of whiskey and sleeping pills to bed with him.

One evening Hal Carter took a cab to the hotel to collect them and found that Eddie was drunk. Hal poured black coffee down him and laid him out on the floor of his dressing room. The Wildcats dressed him and lifted him up, put a guitar around his neck, put on his dark glasses, stood him behind the curtains and hoped for the best. They hoped that the adrenalin would kick in once he heard the applause. It did but halfway through the scheduled set, he fell to his knees but continued playing. Hal Carter pulled the curtains across and they lifted him up and he continued as though it was an encore. Big Jim Sullivan: "Eddie and Gene used to drink a bottle of bourbon before they went on stage. They were the first men I'd ever seen who really drank. They drank shorts so they weren't like beer drinkers. Eddie was so drunk at the Liverpool Empire that we weren't sure that he'd make it to the stage. It had one of those microphones hat comes up from the floor. We positioned Eddie so that it would come up between his body and his guitar and he could balance on it. He sobered up after two songs and untangled himself. He gave a good show, so he never had anything to apologise for."

But Gene did. ASBOs could have been invented for Gene Vincent. Big Jim Sullivan: "I can remember Gene having a go at the stage manager in Liverpool and he had his knife out. I only saw the end of the incident so I don't know what happened, but Gene would go off his head now and again. I've known him to smash up a dressing room because something upset him."

Let's turn to the fans out front. First, David Deacon: "I can remember the evening well as I couldn't believe it. They looked so fabulous and they were everything that we thought American rock'n'roll should be. They were competent, very exciting and they looked great. I was especially impressed to see Eddie Cochran in his leathers."

John Cochrane: "I remember having high expectations as I worshipped Gene and Eddie. It was a great show but it would have been enough to have been in the same building as them."

Mick O'Toole: "I went to the show with some lads and we were surrounded by girls who were screaming their heads off. I felt like standing up and saying, 'Why don't you listen to it?' as we were there for the music. The girls, I suppose, were there for different reasons. I thought Billy Fury's business of wrapping himself around the microphone and rolling on the floor was well over the top, especially for a British artist as the British were a lot more staid and reserved than the Americans. I thought Eddie Cochran was great and that had he lived, he could have given Elvis a run for his money. He had style and class and excitement. Gene Vincent was exciting in a different way – nobody wanted to be Gene Vincent, but we all wanted to be Eddie Cochran."

While the tour was in Liverpool, the owner of the Jacaranda coffee-bar, Allan Williams told Parnes of his plans to have a huge beat show at Liverpool Stadium. It would star Eddie and Gene and would feature other Parnes' acts as well as the cream of local talent. Williams was hyping it up but Parnes was intrigued to learn about the burgeoning of local talent. The concert was set for 3 May 1960.

The week at Liverpool Empire was followed by another at Manchester Hippodrome. They went to Manchester by train and Eddie kept filling up Billy's glass. He told him that the white stones on the track were snow and when the train arrived at Manchester, Billy dropped between the coaches. He clutched a handful of the mineral and said triumphantly, "See, Eddie, I told you they were stones." He was also involved in childish pranks with Gene and Eddie, notably hiding away the shoes that other hotel guests had left outside their rooms to be cleaned. They celebrated by singing 'My Old Man's A Dustman' together. Bobby Darin, who was touring with Duane Eddy around the same time, shared this passion for switching shoes around. At other times, Eddie would dismantle a stool and put it back together and they would laugh as it collapsed when somebody sat on it.

Eddie Cochran was pursued by the Los Angeles songwriter, Sharon Sheeley, who had written 'Poor Little Fool' for Ricky Nelson and also 'Somethin' Else' for Eddie. Sharon Sheeley was the ultimate groupie girl. She had met Ricky Nelson by feigning car trouble in front of his house. She cornered Elvis Presley at the Knickerbocker Hotel in Los Angeles and she hugged Phil Everly after a concert. Eddie enjoyed his freedom and did not want to be tied down, but Sharon was determined. During one late night call when Cochran was lonely, he suggested that she came over for her birthday. She took it as an invitation, paid her own fare and joined the tour, much to Eddie's chagrin.

Hal Carter: "Before Sharon Sheeley arrived, Eddie told me that she was a 'great-looking chick'. When I first met her, I said to Eddie, 'I thought you said she was good-looking.' Eddie thought that was a huge joke, but Sharon didn't appreciate it at all."

NME journalist, Keith Goodwin: "Sharon Sheeley was absolutely devoted to Eddie. Her eyes would light up as soon as she saw him. I never really found out what he thought about her, but I don't think that he wanted to be tied down."

The well-known Levi's 501 ad from 1988 in which Sharon wins Eddie with her jeans was fantasy. Hal Carter: "Eddie had a lot of girlfriends and was a free agent, but he didn't want to hurt Sharon's feelings. He would buy her flowers when he had hurt her feelings. He would say, 'I'm a goddam asshole.'"

Brian Bennett: "Sharon was a lovely, quiet girl who could talk about music. Eddie used to call her 'Charlie Brown'." Jack Good was similarly impressed – he liked her name, her looks and her songwriting and he did cut a single with her for Decca called, appropriately enough, 'Homesick'. In view of what happened, it was never released.

Eddie and Sharon were said to be 'unofficially engaged' whatever that might mean, but the evidence suggests that Sharon was often on her own – or with Billy. Hal Carter: "I can confirm that Billy had an affair with Sharon Sheeley. I'm fairly certain that Eddie didn't know about it, although it wouldn't have bothered him if he did."

Sharon could see that Gene was a bad influence on Eddie and that he got in the way of their friendship. Gene was ill during the week and missed a couple of dates, the official reason being pleurisy. No such thing: it was a bout of heavy drinking. The balladeer Peter Wynne stood in. He hadn't had any hits but his cover of 'Twilight Time' had received some airplay. Gene was grateful and said that Peter should stay on for the rest of the week, and then for the rest of the tour. He was allocated two songs in each perform-ance.

In Gene's absence, the running order changed and Eddie closed the show. Eddie was introduced as "The Rock'n'Roll Legend from the United States". The curtains parted and the lights picked out the singer with his back to the audience. The backing group started and the music pounded to a crescendo and Eddie spun round, guitar swinging and went into 'Somethin' Else'. He and Jim Sullivan had also worked out a little dance routine across the stage. A girl threw him a red rose which he put on the end of his guitar.

Eddie and Gene were staying in the Milverton Lodge, Manchester and Eddie had bought several of Buddy Holly's records and was playing them over and over. He regarded the UK No.1, Johnny Preston's version of the Big Bopper's song, 'Running Bear', as some kind of sign. On the Thursday morning, Eddie, looking pale and drawn, told the hotel manager Arnold Burlin, "I feel so horrible, there is nothing I can do about it, but I know I am going to die.' He did the same on Friday and Saturday but he got some sleep as a doctor prescribed some sedatives.

Larry Parnes: "Two or three times I heard Eddie say he was on borrowed time. He felt that he could have been in that crash which killed Buddy Holly. I remember driving from one date to another and Vince Eager was driving his Triumph. Suddenly, Vince had to swerve to avoid a truck and Eddie said, 'There you are. It could have been today.'"

Jim Sullivan: "Eddie was cut up about Buddy Holly's death but he didn't talk about it much. He would disappear when he felt bad. I did see him crying one night in his dressing room. Maybe it was brought on by the booze, but when I asked him what was wrong, he said, 'I had a dream about Buddy last night.'"

When Gene became drunk, he could be vicious and he and Eddie had a playful fight. Eddie got Gene on the run. Gene scrambled over a bed to get away and put his arm out to keep Eddie away. Eddie got his eye in the way and had a black shiner.

On Friday April 1, Eddie made a personal appearance at The Record Shop in Hilton Street, Stevenson Square, Manchester. Eddie wore dark glasses to hide his black eye, but he turned it to his advantage when he got on stage. The fans shouted, "Take your glasses off" and he would lift them up slightly and go "Uh huh". He was so pleased with the effect that he used the glasses after the eye had healed.

After the two shows that night, Eddie and Gene together with Joe Brown and Billy Fury went to the Oldham Carnival Ball and saw the crowning of Margaret Swords as the Carnival Queen. The judges included Bill Grundy, then with Granada's 'People And Places' and later to conduct a notorious, live interview with the Sex Pistols. There is a photograph from around this time of Eddie with a carnival fortune teller: her reading may have heightened his insecurity.

Jack Good arrived on Saturday afternoon and found them both in bed. Gene had a hangover and Eddie, suffering from insomnia, had strained eyes. What's more, Joe Brown had lost his voice and Billy Fury was suffering from overwork. They still put on a good show and Jack wrote about it in 'Disc'. However, Eddie didn't mention his problems to him: "I never saw Eddie with a sense of doom and if he thought he was going to die, why did he release 'Three Steps To Heaven'? Buddy Holly's final record was 'It Doesn't Matter Anymore' and surely he would have looked at it in the same light if he felt that way."

On Sunday 3 April 1960, Gene and Eddie returned to London and stayed at the Stratford Court Hotel, which is just off Oxford Street. Norm Riley was based there when he was in town.

There was almost a rock'n'roll festival at the Finsbury Park Empire as it was Gene Vincent and Eddie Cochran (week of April 4), Duane Eddy (week of April 11) and Johnny Preston (week of April 25). Billy Fury and Joe Brown had left the tour and the line-up was Gene Vincent, Eddie Cochran, Tony Sheridan, Georgie Fame, Peter Wynne, Dean Webb and compère Billy Raymond. Raymond wanted to leave as he was fed up with Gene's behaviour. Dean Webb was another young British rocker, who had recorded 'Hey

Miss Fanny' (how about that for innuendo?) the previous year. The 'Tottenham Herald' said that the balladeer Peter Wynne "will be a star long after Eddie Cochran and Gene Vincent are forgotten." We're still waiting.

Adrian Owlett, who became Gene's road manager in late 60s, recalled: "I met them in a sandwich bar when they were rehearsing for the Finsbury Park Empire show in 1960. Gene was very, very polite and very friendly, courteous to a fault. He asked where we were from and which house we were going to. I had the impression that he would have been happy to spend the whole day talking about rock'n'roll. Cochran was ill, but he seemed like a Hollywood star. He believed that a star should be a star at all times, and even though it was only 11 in the morning, he was wearing make-up."

The opening night at Finsbury Park Empire was Sharon Sheeley's twentieth birthday. Hal Carter: "Sharon was besotted with Eddie, but he was a playboy. All the girls liked him. She wasn't with him all the time when she was over here. She'd go off sightseeing, and Billy Fury fell in love with her. He had invited her to come over because he was homesick and lonely. I couldn't see him getting married though, not for a long time, until he had got it all out of his system." Eddie asked another road manager on the tour, Patrick Thompkins, to buy a huge birthday cake. Sharon said that she only needed a small one and she used the rest of the money to get Eddie a blue corduroy shirt.

After the concert on Tuesday night, Eddie, Sharon and another touring group, Duane Eddy and the Rebels, went to the Condor Club to see Terry Dene performing. "When we got back from the club," she recalled, "Duane went to bed and Eddie and I sat in the hotel lobby. We ordered and drank three bottles of champagne." They stayed up so late that a chambermaid appeared with a vacuum cleaner. Eddie asked the maid to lend him her cap and vacuum and he knocked on Duane's door. He started to clean up and was saying, 'My goodness, Mr Eddy, you're very untidy, aren't you?'

Gene and Eddie also met the Everly Brothers and the Crickets, who were touring with the Everlys. Eddie told Jerry Allison of the Crickets, "If I'd known you guys were coming over here, I'd have had you bring me a bottle of American air."

Clive Selwood: "Phil Everly came backstage to see Eddie Cochran and he brought a couple of guns and holsters with him. They had a quick draw contest just like you see in 'The Magnificent Seven'. They stood a couple of feet apart: I stood in the middle and when I clapped my hands, they drew together."

Gene and Eddie shared a room with twin beds and one night they returned, drunk, with some girls. They had forgotten the key so they kicked down the door. When the manager came to investigate, he found them all in bed with the door hanging from the bottom hinge. The next day Keith Goodwin of the NME interviewed them in the hotel and described them as "quiet, polite and unspoiled." They were both fans of Brenda Lee and loved her record, 'Sweet Nuthin's'. Cochran commented that some fans had travelled round the country to see them at different venues, an unusual occurrence at the time. "Most of our journeys are by train," said Vincent, "I don't like British trains. They're not comfortable."

Eddie was doing 'Somethin' Else' as his opener. The spotlight would hit his back and he would turn around with a "Now look-a here." Eddie was making circular movements with his guitar, which mimicked the pistons of a steam engine.

Licorice Locking: "I loved doing 'Hallelujah I Love Her So' with Eddie as we would play the solo back to back. He was a great looking feller, but I'll always remember him with bloodshot eyes. During that week in London, I played harmonica in Eddie's dressing room and he was quite impressed. He said that we were going to do some blues together when he came back."

Cochran was far more comfortable than Gene at talking to the audience, but Gene had a line with hecklers. If someone shouted, "Get on with it", he would say, "Son, I could make a fool of you but your ma and pa beat me to it."

On stage, Gene was doing very well with Jack Scott's 'What In The World's Come Over You'. He was definitely appealing to the rockers but he could hold them spellbound with 'Over The Rainbow', which he sang in a trance. They concluded with duets of 'What'd I Say' and 'Shake, Rattle And Roll'.

Larry Parnes; "I had been there on the opening night and I went to see two or three more, and I felt that the show was a damp squid after Eddie had performed. Gene was a wonderful performer but he was a slower performer and Eddie had an aura about him, something that the audience wanted. I held a meeting with Eddie and Gene and discussed the problem. We had sold out but I wanted the audience to enjoy every minute of the show. I felt that we should put Eddie into the second half, then Billy and then Gene but that didn't work because it ruined the first half. I could have closed the first half with Gene and he wasn't against it at all, especially as I told him that we could drop the finale and he could get away earlier. However, Eddie said that he wouldn't do it because Gene was the star of the show and he had come into the show after Gene, so it stayed the way it was."

When Eddie Cochran was featured in the love comic for girls, 'Valentine', he wrote, "Best always to the readers of 'Valentine'. Don't forget me, Eddie Cochran."

Daily Mirror

MON APR. 16 1960

No. 17,522

2ᵈ

'ROCK' STAR DIES IN CRASH

● PICTURED ABOVE: Singer Eddie Cochran. LEFT: The wreckage of the car after the crash which killed him.

Above;
Johnny Gentle, who
had to siphon petrol
out of the car wreck
that killed Eddie in
order to get back
home

By NED GRANT

AMERICAN rock 'n' roll singing star Eddie Cochran, 21, died yesterday after a car taking him to London Airport crashed.

Among the three other passengers in the car when it crashed at Chippenham, Wilts, on Saturday night were two Americans—"rock" singer Gene Vincent, 25, and girl song writer Sharon Sheeley, 20.

Last night Miss Sheeley—she wrote the hit song "Poor Little Fool" when she was seventeen—was in "fair" condition with a fractured pelvis in hospital at Bath, Somerset.

Her mother, Mrs. Mary Sheeley, added in Hollywood last night when she heard of the crash.

The news was broken to Mrs. Sheeley by the mother of Ritchie Valens—the "rock" star who was killed at the age of sixteen last year in an air crash soon after revealing that it Sharon's own engagement...

going steady since they met two cats ago.

Eddie was the first and only boy friend Sharon ever had. They were terribly in love, and were planning to marry. They were unofficially engaged.

The car's driver, George Martin, of Harlcliffe, Bristol, was unhurt.

Cochran—with Sharon, Gene Vincent and the fourth passenger Campbell, theatrical agent Patrick Thomkins, 26—was taken to hospital.

America-bound

Just after four o'clock yesterday afternoon, Cochran died. Cochran's record hits have included "Summertime Blues" and "C'mon Everybody"—was travelling from Bristol where he was starring in variety to catch an America-bound plane at London Airport.

He had been in Britain since January, appearing on the stage and in TV shows—including ITV's Boy Meets Girls—with Gene Vincent, whose first big song hit was "Be-Bop-A-Lula," planned to fly with Cochran.

He said to hospital last night: "I hope to be out in two or three days."

Cochran's last record was ...

The toll: 33 dead 632 injured

AT least thirty-three people have been killed and 632 injured on the roads since the Easter Holiday started on Good Friday.

And last night the Automobile Association made an urgent Bank Holiday appeal for safety on the roads.

First reports of YESTERDAY'S ACCIDENTS showed that for the...

people was stations into Previous... GOOD F SATURDAY by the Assault Twenty-on 616 injured. Last year s same tw Fifteen injured. ... their night, th

These ... then s gist of thousand... An all n...

Sharon Sheeley

TRAGEDY

TRAGEDY STRUCK the world of rock 'n' roll on Easter Sunday, when American performer Eddie Cochran—who had just ended a tour of Britain —died in St. Martin's Hospital, Bath, where he had been taken a few hours earlier after being in a car crash.

It was the most shattering news to reach fans of beat music since the deaths in a plane crash last year of Buddy Holly, Big Bopper and Ritchie Valens.

Cochran had completed his British tour at Bristol on Easter Saturday night, and was in a chauffeur-driven hire car headed for London Airport.

There he was due to take a plane back to America, to help in the promotion of his new disc release, "Three Steps To Heaven."

Also in the car were Sharon Sheeley, a songwriter, who was a close friend of Cochran's; Gene Vincent, another American beat singer, who had been appearing with him and agent Patrick Thompkins. They suffered comparatively minor injuries, and—at the time of going to press— were reported as "comfortable."

Vince Eager, British rock performer, had been waiting at the airport to fly to America with Cochran—as his guest. When he heard the news, he cancelled his flight, and was planning to travel in the plane that took Cochran's body back to America for burial.

INQUEST IS ADJOURNED

AT THE INQUEST AT BATH on Tuesday, the coroner was informed that brain injuries in the car crash had killed Eddie Cochran, who was only 21 years of age. The inquest was adjourned until May 23. Cochran's body was flown home on Wednesday from London Airport to his home in Hollywood. Latest news about GENE VINCENT and SHARON SHEELEY, who were with Cochran in the same car when it crashed, is that they are

DID Eddie Cochran know that he was going to die? Did he, in some mysterious way, foresee the tragic car crash that was to end his life at the very moment when it was starting to show its greatest promise?

There is little doubt that he was going through a temporary black spell—a feeling of depression unusual in a boy who was always so fun-loving.

Only a few days before the crash the U.S. rock 'n' roll star

1960, could hardly have happened at a more tragic moment.

For one thing, he was on his way to London Airport, eagerly looking forward to a few days home in California.

Even more important, he was to have been married in Hollywood the following Saturday—to 20-year-old Sharon Sheeley, the girl he had been secretly engaged to for two years, and who was with him in the car.

His death, coming shortly after the loss of Buddy Holly, was a severe blow to the music industry, for he was undoubtedly one of the most talented newcomers.

A dynamic singer, a first-rate guitarist, a prolific composer and a promising actor, Eddie was generally agreed to be just at the start of a

Flashback to NME Poll-winners' Concert, 1960.

EDDIE COCHRAN
born October 3, 1938
died April 27, 1960

A TRAGIC LOSS
TO POP MUSIC

had to remain unfulfilled.

Despite his great wealth of talent, Eddie remained a modest, easy-going, unspoilt boy at heart.

"He really enjoyed life," his manager Norm Riley recalls. "He had simple tastes, liked the open air, and rarely found anything to complain about. You simply couldn't dislike Eddie."

Eddie used to say that the biggest drawback of being a star was not having time to see his old friends.

"**Back home I like to hang around with a gang of old buddies, but the publicity men don't like this. They get mad at me, and say I go out with the wrong people.**"

Among the people who got to know him best were the rock stars who worked alongside him. They remember him as a fine artist, a loyal friend—and an outsize leg-puller.

Like the morning he borrowed a cap and cleaner from the hotel maid, burst into Duane Eddy's room and, as he started to clean up, said: "My goodness, Mr. Eddy, you're very untidy, aren't you?"

Nowhere was his loss more keenly felt than among his fans. The handsome American in his fur-lined black leather jacket and leather trousers had become a familiar figure during the months he spent in Britain.

In the weeks following his death, tributes poured in from countless thousands of fans who had come to recognise him as one of the most exciting disc personalities of his time.

Above all, in their response to his later recordings, they seemed determined to keep his memory alive.

It wasn't long before the ironically titled "Three Steps To Heaven" became a best-seller, reaching No. 2 spot during its long run in the charts and becoming as big a hit as any Eddie had enjoyed during his lifetime.

There was a big demand, too, for the "Eddie Cochran Memorial Album," a new LP including many of his past hits, which was released here in September.

But that is by no means the end of the Eddie Cochran story.

Liberty, his American label, has a further stockpile of at least 20 titles which it considers up to the standard Eddie would have insisted on.

Their release in the coming months will ensure that Eddie's name remains a dominant force in popular music.

In the words of the girl he was engaged to:

"Eddie Cochran is not dead. He is away on a long tour, and it won't be long before I see him again."

By the way they have kept his records spinning, it looks as if his many thousands of fans feel the same way about him.

admitted that he had been suffering from a bout of insomnia.

No doubt he was also feeling the effects of the hectic schedule of concerts, variety and TV shows since he arrived in Britain.

He was pretty homesick, too, after this first visit overseas.

"It's been pretty tough these last few weeks," he told the NME a few days before his death.

"**I'm so homesick that I feel I just have to get back to the States for a few days.**"

Then there was the incident at Manchester which was kept secret at the time, but leaked out soon after he died.

One night Eddie suddenly woke up in the small hours and ran screaming to the hotel manager's room. Pounding on the door, he shouted: "I'm going to die. I know I'm going to die."

The crash that came on that dark, lonely road on April 17.

great show business career.

As his American recording chief, Alvin Bennett, has said: "He was only just getting started. Sure, he had some hits, but he had by no means reached his peak.

"I'm sure he was destined to become one of the all-time greats of beat music."

Eddie first came to prominence as a Hollywood studio musician. Singing came later—by accident. After a snap audition, he won a minor rôle in the big-beat film, "The Girl Can't Help It."

A contract with Liberty Records followed, and soon he was hitting the high spots with million-plus sales of his own compositions, "Twenty Flight Rock" and "Sittin' In The Balcony."

His first British success, "Summertime Blues," which enjoyed a lengthy spell in the charts in 1958, was a fine example of his versatility. Besides writing and

arranging the tune, he was also featured, by multi-recording techniques, on piano, bass, guitar and drums.

Later came "C'mon Everybody," "Somethin' Else" and—to coincide with his arrival in Britain early in the year—"Hallelujah, I Love Her So."

Meanwhile, his screen career was blossoming. Impressed with his first movie appearance, producers signed him for further guest spots in "Untamed," with Mamie Van Doren, and "Bop Girl."

Eddie was really keen to make the grade as an actor.

"I'd like to get down to some serious acting when the right story and part come along," he said.

One of the things he had planned to do on his return to the States was to discuss a big dramatic movie rôle. This ambition

9. OPEN UP THAT GOLDEN GATE
Bristol, April 1960

"Why don't you people learn to drive,
You know you just might stay alive."
(Gene Vincent, LP track, 1959)

After a successful week at the Finsbury Park Empire, Gene and Eddie took a train to Bristol on Sunday 10 April 1960 for a week of concerts at the Hippodrome. Eddie was fascinated by the communication cord and the notice said that the penalty for improper use was £5. He pulled it a couple of times and when the guard came to see what the trouble was, Eddie was there, smiling, with a £5 note. Eddie and Gene were staying together in Suite 105 of the Grand Hotel, Bristol. It was known as the Cary Grant Suite as Grant stayed there when he visited his home town.

Following the week in Bristol, Eddie Cochran would return to Los Angeles for a few days and he had booked some studio time with his producer, Snuff Garrett at Liberty. He wanted to make what would be his second album. He also planned to record some instrumentals with a young Glen Campbell as well as working with his British friend, Vince Eager. Vince, who was playing in Scotland that week in April, was looking forward to the sessions: it was rare for a British performer to record in America.

Gene Vincent was booked to appear at the Alhambra Theatre in Paris from Easter Sunday, but quite possibly he had no intention of fulfilling these dates. It wouldn't have been for Parnes so Parnes wouldn't have put pressure on him. Instead, he planned to go back to America with Eddie. He hadn't been home since December and his relationship with Darlene in the UK had been stormy, to say the least? Was he going home to patch it up? We will never know.

Gene and Eddie would reunite at the end of the month and the tour was set for Hanley, Lewisham, Cheltenham, Salisbury, Guildford, Halifax, Chester, Wolverhampton and Romford. Although nothing had been announced, Parnes had plans for presenting Gene and Vince Eager in a summer season at the Queen's Theatre, Blackpool. Larry Parnes: "It was very easy to arrange a further tour, although people were starting to take notice of Eddie again in the States because he was doing so well over here. Gene had nothing in the States at all." It's hard to say why Eddie accepted this. Gene, I suspect, would have clung to Eddie and begged him to do the tour.

Hal Carter: "Eddie never made any business calls but he did ring Jerry Capehart who was his friend and business manager. He wasn't happy about what Jerry had done for him in the past, but he never complained he had been ripped off or anything like that. He wasn't terribly interested in making money. He agreed to do a further 10 weeks in the UK and then he wanted me to go back to America with him as his manager."

Jack Good had devised yet another TV show, his fourth, and this time it was 'Wham!' He wanted both Billy Fury and Joe Brown for the opening programmes and so he arranged for Joe and Billy to rehearse with him that week in April, and Hal Carter was assigned to them. The road manager to complete this leg of the tour was another Parnes employee, 29-year-old Patrick Thompkins. The revised supporting bill for the week in Bristol was Tony Sheridan, Georgie Fame, Peter Wynne and Billy Raymond. Marty Wilde needed the Wildcats for some gigs and so both Gene and Eddie were backed by the Beat Boys with Georgie Fame. Later in the week, the Liverpool balladeer Johnny Gentle arrived by car and joined the tour.

This time Eddie entered to the strummed introduction of 'C'mon Everybody' and he moved across the stage. When he reached the centre, he had a spot on him and the rest of the stage was in darkness. He looked at the audience and the music stopped and he took off his dark glasses. The girls screamed and he began to sing. Eddie said to one heckler, "Would somebody put a lid on that trash can over there?" The 'Bristol Evening Post' was intrigued by Vincent's crouching position: "His act is conducted almost entirely in a bent almost double position, like a motor-cyclist lying over the handle bars. This puts his diaphragm at its greatest disadvantage". So now you know.

Keith Goodwin: "I always wanted to hear Eddie play more guitar. I thought he was a good singer but he was a very powerful, provocative guitar player. I saw him at Bristol a couple of nights before he died and I told him that I'd like to see him do a couple of instrumentals on stage. He said, 'Well, maybe later in the year.' He really liked playing in England and he liked playing live. The next day I was rung up by a colleague in Fleet Street and told the news. It was as shattering to me as the death of Judy Garland or the lunatic who shot John Lennon."

The show played to good houses on the Monday to Thursday but the theatre was not permitted to open on Good Friday. It was a good Friday as Patrick Thompkins gave Eddie and Gene their tickets for America.

The second house on Saturday was at 8.40 and the actor Peter Bowles was at that last show. He was resident with the Bristol Old Vic but he was free that Saturday night. "The stage was in complete darkness and the spotlight came on as the music started, but it was on Eddie Cochran's bum. He was wearing tight red leather trousers, I'd never seen anything like that before, and his bottom was gyrating. This was sexy and the audience was screaming. He also said, 'I'm gonna do something I've never done before' and I thought, we all thought, 'He's going to drop his pants', and then he said, 'I'm gonna smile' and we all went raving mad."

The curtain fell at around 10.40pm and both Eddie and Gene were on stage for the encore. Eddie and Gene embraced and the tour was over, at least for a fortnight.

Before we detail what happened next, I would like to consider what was meant to happen. You could go to America by boat or plane, but it was only in 1958 that more people crossed the Atlantic by air rather than sea for the first time. Even so there were only three flights from London Airport (now Heathrow) to New York on that Sunday, Easter Sunday. They were:

BOAC – Flight BC509. This was a 707 which left at 1pm and arrived in New York at 3.20pm their time.

TWA – Frankfurt 3pm, London 4.25pm with departure at 5.30pm, New York 8.25pm.

Pan-Am – Frankfurt 3.30pm, London 4.55pm with departure at 6pm, New York 8.55pm

Although Air India flew this route, there was no Sunday service.

The BOAC flight at 1pm was chosen, which meant that passengers had to check in by noon.

Eddie, Gene and Sharon were going back with Vince Eager. Eddie had spoken to Vince during the week. He was on tour in Scotland and he had arranged to meet them at Gene's flat in Fulham at 8.30am on the Sunday morning. In other words, they were not planning to stay in Bristol overnight. Larry Parnes: "Eddie and Gene and Vince Eager were going back to America. I felt it was best that they should take the last train from Bristol to London, which left just after midnight and bookings had been made for them. I had arranged for a car to meet them in London to take them to the Stratford Court Hotel and then there was another car to take them in the morning to the airport. This was going to give them about four hours' sleep. They were the ones who had chosen to take the plane at lunchtime and not wait until the evening. If they'd followed my arrangements, everything would have been all right."

The last evening train from Bristol Temple Meads to London was the 7.40pm so they could not have caught that. A mail train left at 1am, but with no public access. However, they could have caught the Penzance to Paddington sleeper. This left Penzance at 8.45pm, departed from Bristol Temple Meads at 3.55am, and arrived in Paddington at 7.25am. As well as sleeping car passengers, the train was also available with standard seating and the buffet stayed open all night to provide some comfort. Not exactly rock star comfort and hardly a preferred option.

The sleeper was the only viable choice if they were going by rail. The first of the Sunday daytime services departed from Bristol Temple Meads at 9am, calling at Reading at 11.04am and arriving at Paddington at 11.52am. It was a three hour journey to London, but there were no high speed trains then. They could alight at Reading and take a cab to the airport but that would be cutting things fine, and one short delay could mean that they would miss the flight.

And it could be a long delay as there was a further complication that

Easter Sunday. The annual Aldermaston march was taking place whereby protesters assembled outside the atomic warheads establishment, again just outside Reading. This would have added travelling time if going by road and also many of the protesters would be travelling by train. The march concluded with a mass rally at Trafalgar Square. The participants included Michael Foot and Canon Collins and there was a lengthy traffic queue as the marchers walked near London Airport. For all these reasons, trains were out, especially as Eddie wanted to collect some presents from the Stratford Court Hotel.

After the show, Eddie and Gene wanted to get back to London. Johnny Gentle: "I wasn't officially on the tour but as one of the singers was sick, Larry asked me to get over to Bristol. I jumped in my car and took my girl-friend and also Peter Wynne and his girlfriend as Peter was also on the bill. Eddie asked me if I could take him, Sharon and Gene back to London, but I couldn't because I'd got a full car. Sharon was standing next to him, saying 'Please'. I would have taken them if I hadn't got a full load. He said he would hire a cab." Gentle's party found a restaurant open after the second house and didn't hit the road until after midnight.

Patrick Thompkins had used a cab firm to take the stars the short journey from the hotel to the theatre. He asked a cab driver how much it would cost to go to London and was told £30. Someone called George Martin (oddly enough) offered to take them in his Ford Consul. There was confetti in the car as it had been used for a wedding earlier in the day. Eddie had left his leather jeans under a mattress at the Grand and had forgotten to pack them. A porter from the hotel ran over to the Hippodrome with them.

Ray McVay: "I was going to go back with Eddie and Gene on that final night. I was in the front ready to go back, but Eddie wanted to get his amp into the car. He was very fond of his amp and he wanted to take it back to America as it needed some attention. I said, 'It's okay, put the amp in the car and I'll travel in the Dormobile with the rest of the boys.'"

Tony Sheridan: "I was a bit pissed off that night as I was staying in Bristol and I would have preferred going to London with my idols."

Hal Carter: "If I'd been there that night, the accident would never have happened. A taxi driver had quoted £30 to take them to London but they thought it was a bit steep and used George Martin instead. He took a wrong turning just before the bridge at Chippenham and he was heading back to Bristol when the accident occurred."

The party got into the Ford Consul saloon, George Martin was driving and Patrick Thompkins was alongside him. Gene, Eddie and Sharon were sat in the back. Eddie was in the middle as Sharon couldn't stand Gene. Gene, however, had taken a sleeping pill and he fell asleep almost immediately. It was a clear and fine night for driving.

Two fans at the stage door assumed that they were going to a hotel and followed them at considerable speed for three miles. Then they hit the Bath road and knew that they weren't staying in Bristol. In order to avoid the lorries, Martin was going to Bath and then from Bath to the market town of Chippenham, Wiltshire. Eddie and Sharon were singing 'California Here I Come'. The song was associated with Al Jolson but in 1955, it had been used to great comic effect in the sitcom, 'I Love Lucy'.

Around 11.50pm, Martin saw the sign A4 but he was going the wrong way and Thompkins pointed this out. Martin was travelling over 40mph in a built-up area, known as Rowden Hill. He braked hard, the tyre burst and the car started sliding. The car hit the kerb on the other side of the road and skidded backwards until it crashed sideways into a concrete lamppost. George Martin told the court: "The car radio was on, the passengers were singing, and I was listening. After I had gone under the railway bridge, I can remember approaching a bend and, as I was about to take it, the car started going out of control for no reason at all."

The rear door was smashed. Eddie was sitting in the middle of the back seat and he threw himself to his left to protect Sharon. His head hit the roof, probably causing his injuries, and the car continued to spin and when the door gave way, he was thrown on to the road.

Sharon Sheeley: "Gene was asleep, which is probably what saved his life. Eddie reached over to cover me. I came to, lying in a cow pasture, bleeding and dazed. I went to move and I couldn't because my neck was broken. Gene crawled over to me and I asked, 'How's Eddie?' Gene said he was OK, just shaken up a bit. I knew then that he was badly injured. Otherwise, Eddie would have crawled over to me himself."

A motor engineer, John Kingman lived by the scene of the accident: "My wife and I were in the lounge, just about to go to bed, when we heard the crash into the lamppost. I got my old army greatcoat and put it over Eddie Cochran and my wife got her coat and put it over the girl, who just kept crying, 'Where's Eddie?' Gene Vincent was already smoking a cigarette and cursing and yelling because he had this massive bump on his head."

A local couple, Dick and Phyllis Jennings were driving home and they made the injured as comfortable as possible until the ambulance came. The driver and passengers were all taken to St Martin's Hospital in Bath. Eddie Cochran had few external injuries but it was quickly recognised that he had severe brain damage. Sharon had a broken pelvis and Gene fractured his collarbone as well as damaging his leg further. George Martin and Patrick Thompkins were shaken but otherwise uninjured.

After eating, Johnny Gentle and his party had set off for London: "It was after midnight and I was out of petrol. There weren't all-night garages then and we asked a policeman if he could help us. He told us that there had been an accident and there was a breakdown truck that might give us the petrol. The driver said we could siphon off the petrol from the wreck, so that's what we did and drove home. It wasn't until the next day that I realised it had been Eddie Cochran's taxi." I didn't believe this remarkable story at first but I asked a policeman from the 1960s who told me that it was totally plausible: he had known it to be done.

Among the police on the scene was a cadet, David Harman. He retrieved Eddie's Gretsch guitar which was unharmed and took it to the station. Also in the guitar case was Sharon's handwritten lyric for 'Cherished Memories'. The guitar was subsequently returned to the Cochran family and Harman later became Dave Dee of Dave Dee, Dozy, Beaky, Mick and Tich. "I was a 17-year-old police cadet in Wiltshire and they took me to as many accidents as they could find. I'd seen loads of accidents by the time of the Eddie Cochran crash and I remember going to the spot. The car had hit a lamppost. Sharon was in the front seat with the driver, Eddie had gone through the windscreen and Gene was in the back. The extraordinary thing was that Eddie's Gretsch guitar had landed in the road and it wasn't damaged at all. We took it back to the police station and it was there for about two months I played it from time to time. I've always felt sorry for the driver because he has had to live with that death for the rest of his life."

Vince Eager had been playing in Scotland and he flew to Birmingham on Easter Saturday. He went to his home in Grantham and then drove to London with his friend and driver, Noel Wallace. He had arranged to meet them at Gene's flat in Fulham at 8.30am on Easter Sunday. There was no one there and Vince waited until 9.15am, hoping that they would turn up. Calling the Stratford Court Hotel, Vince spoke to Norm Riley who said that they had probably gone to a party and would go straight to the airport. Vince got there shortly after 10am. He went into Pan-Am's VIP lounge and he was sitting next to Count Basie, who had cancelled some dates on his UK tour as his father had died.

Vince was paged by Danny Sutherton, who was Larry Parnes' press agent. He told him that there had been an accident, that Gene was not too good but Eddie would be discharged tomorrow. Vince decided to continue with his flight as he was meeting his brother the next day in New York. He got on the plane, only to be called back by another message, this time from Larry Parnes. Parnes told him that Eddie was dying. Vince got his luggage off the plane, found that his driver Noel Wallace and his car were still around and drove to Bath as quickly as he could, arriving at 1.30pm.

According to Vince, the surgeon told him that Eddie was very ill and unlikely to survive. (Doctors do not normally say such things to non-relatives, but there were no relatives around.) Vince saw Gene who had fractured his collarbone, damaged his elbow and was badly cut behind his ear. Gene's fantasies were working overtime. He told a doctor, "I'll give you £1m if you can save Eddie's life." He later told reporters that he had a brain surgeon flown in, and although he operated, Eddie died. In reality, it was planned to move Eddie to the Frenchay Hospital in Bristol, which specialised in brain injuries but he was too weak to move. There was much internal haemorrhaging and he never regained consciousness. Eddie Cochran died at 4.10pm.

Sharon Sheeley: "I kept going in and out of consciousness asking, 'How is Eddie?' At four o'clock, this stranger took my hand and said, 'I'm very sorry. He's passed away.' It's not like in the movies. You don't scream. The scream is so deep in your guts: it won't come out of your own throat.'

Larry Parnes, Norm Riley, Billy Fury and Dickie Pride arrived together at 2pm. Parnes assumed control and was already spinning the accident, saying how ironic it was that Eddie's next record should be 'Three Steps To Heaven'. Vince Eager was disgusted and told Parnes he would never work for him again – and he never did. Vince did think of flying with the body to the States, but fearing that Parnes would make capital of it, he changed his mind. Nevertheless, the tabloids did run stories of 'Pop Star To Fly Back With Pal's Coffin', which was Parnes once again at work.

Georgie Fame: "On the last night of the tour, we went back to London in a Dormobile with some of the musicians: Ray McVay was driving. We left after Eddie's taxi but we didn't see anything and the next day we had a gig as a band in Southend. We all met at Newbury Park tube station for the pick-up at lunchtime. We didn't know anything had happened."

Tim Rice: "I remember Easter Sunday 1960 and having supper with my brothers. My father had been listening to the radio and he asked us if we had heard of Eddie Cochran. We were amazed that our father had brought Eddie Cochran into the conversation or, for that matter, any pop singer. He wasn't even aware of Elvis, really. He told us that he had been killed and that was a really bad moment: tears around the baked beans on toast."

Licorice Locking had been playing with Marty Wilde with the Wildcats: "We had finished on the Saturday and I was travelling on Sunday to get home. I got home at about 6pm and heard about his death on the news. That was the first I had heard about it and I was devastated."

Actress Sue Johnston: "Eddie Cochran was my hero when I was 15 or 16 and I wore a black armband and wept when he died. I still love his records – they are ageless, I think."

Marty Wilde told the press, "Eddie Cochran had a fabulous stage act. He was a raunchy, loose-limbed guy who enjoyed himself. There was nothing pretentious about him. He was an extremely good musician."

Larry Parnes: "A couple of nights before the accident. I had a dream about a hotel room with two beds in it. Gene was about to go and Eddie was standing in the middle of the room, naked except for his guitar and he was strumming it. When I visited Gene in hospital, I told him about my dream and he stopped me and said, 'He was naked except for his guitar'. I said, 'How do you know?' and he said, 'Because it happened.'"

On Easter Sunday, Eddie Cochran's family had gathered together to welcome him home. They heard on the radio that there had been an accident and then a phone call, presumably from Norm Riley, to say he had gone.

On Monday, the 'Daily Mirror' led with the story, "Rock Star Dies In Crash", but the incident wasn't even mentioned in 'The Times', although it did report that 21 people had been killed on the roads in the first two days of the holiday weekend.

Si Waronker of Liberty Records said, "I was at home in bed when the phone rang and woke me up. It broke my heart to hear the news. Then I got a phone call from a DJ here in Los Angeles, who wanted me to comment on the radio. In those days, rock music was just beginning, so these things didn't really make the headlines. It wasn't as important to people as it is today." That Monday night, the Everly Brothers accompanied by the Crickets played the Colston Hall in Bristol. They were accompanied by Cherry Wainer, Lance Fortune, the Dallas Boys and the Flee-Rekkers. The Everly Brothers paid tribute to their good friend, Eddie Cochran.

Sharon Sheeley's mother was given the news in Hollywood. She said, "Eddie Cochran was the first and only boyfriend that Sharon ever had. They were unofficially engaged." She flew over on the Tuesday to see her daughter in hospital. Sharon later said, "Gene was a very sad, pathetic person. He was suicidal, even before the accident. Eddie was such an up guy with so much to live for, and Gene wanted to die. I wondered why God didn't just pick Gene then."

ABC-TV's 'Wham!' was first broadcast on 23 April 1960 and again Jack Good offered something new: rock'n'roll theatre in the round. An audience of 500 circled the performers so they were always in the shot. The opening programme featured Joe Brown, Jess Conrad, Billy Fury, Dickie Pride, Little Tony, the Four Jays and the Vernons Girls. The backing came from an augmented Rockingham XI, now called Jack Good's Fat Noise and led by Red Price. The acts performed complete songs and Billy performed the first versions of Ray Charles' 'What'd I Say' and Barrett Strong's 'Money' on UK television. Each week the viewers were asked to vote for their favourite star but it was something of a 'no contest' as Billy invariably won. Still, the contest showed that Jack Good had sown the seeds for another aspect of 'Pop Idol'.

Gene Vincent discharged himself on the Tuesday, the day that the post mortem was concluded. Gene intended to accompany Eddie's body to the States but he could not book a suitable flight and the body was not released in time. Gene went to America on Wednesday and the body eventually travelled to Los Angeles on Saturday 23 April. He was buried two days later in the Forest Lawn Memorial Park, near Buena Park. There were 250 mourners including Ritchie Valens' mother. There was a wreath of red and white carnations shaped like a guitar. His gravestone includes a poem, which purports to quote God's thoughts:

"We need a master guitarist and singer
I know of but one alone.
His name is Eddie Cochran,
I think I'll call him home."

In the next Friday's NME, Sharon Sheeley, speaking from her hospital bed said, "Eddie and I were officially and secretly engaged two years ago. We told no one because Eddie didn't want his teenage fans to know. We were to be married in Hollywood on Saturday." She was as much a fantasist as Gene Vincent, Norm Riley and Larry Parnes and her views were given full rein in the TV documentary, 'Eddie Cochran – Cherished Memories' (1999). This curious NME feature was balanced by a second one in which she talked about dating Elvis Presley and Ricky Nelson.

On 24 June 1960 at Bristol Assizes, George Martin was found guilty of "causing the death of Edward Ray Cochran by driving dangerously at high speed." He was fined £50 – to be paid off at £5 a year - and disqualified from driving for 15 years.

COCHRAN will hit the top again

EDDIE COCHRAN

Three Steps To Heaven; Cut Across Shorty

(London HLG9115)

D N T

EDDIE COCHRAN was undoubtedly one of the most talented personalities on the beat scene. Like Buddy Holly I think he will go on "enjoying" hit parade success even though he's no longer with us.

His London release of "Three Steps To Heaven" would certainly have registered powerfully if Eddie had been touring still. As it is I must tip the side for chart honours. A solid, romantic beater, well worked out.

Country song on the flip is catchy and amusing.

EDDIE COCHRAN'S LAST RECORD

"THREE Steps To Heaven" is the song sung on a new London release by Eddie Cochran, the American singer who was recently killed in a car crash in the South of England.

It's a medium-paced song with an attractive, beaty rhythm. Accompaniment is on guitars, aided by a vocal group.

"Cut Across Shorty" is a lively and entertaining rock number about some rivals for a girl's affections—but the girl has already made up her mind that Shorty is her man.

VINCENT CUTS COCHRAN DISC

GENE VINCENT last week cut his first disc in England, for distribution here and in the States. At EMI's London studios he recorded "Pistol Packin' Momma" and "Weeping Willow," due for release on June 10.

The arrangements for the A side, "Pistol Packin' Momma," were done specially for Gene by his friend Eddie Cochran a few days before he was tragically killed in a car accident.

TOPTWENTY

Compiled from dealers' returns from all over Britain

Week ending May 7, 1960

Faith now at No. 2.. Eddie Cochran's 'Three Steps To Heaven,' jumps in at No. 16

Last Week	This Week	Title	Artist	Label
1	1	Cathy's Clown	Everly Brothers	Warner Bros
4	2	Someone Else's Baby	Adam Faith	Parlophone
2	3	Do You Mind ?	Anthony Newley	
3	4	Fall In Love With You		

121

Rock star **GENE VINCENT** has had to cut short his British tour—but before he left he gave this interview to DISC reporter Richard Adams.

FIRST IT WAS THE EDDIE COCHRAN TRAGEDY, THEN CAME THE DEATH OF HIS DAUGHTER, MELODY, BUT HIS FANS UNDERSTOOD...

I guess they just felt sorry for me

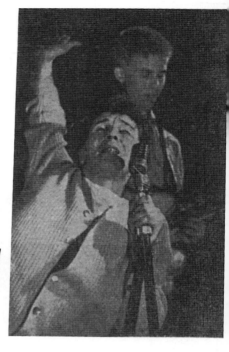

WITH most singers, their voice and face are their fortune. With Gene Vincent it's the same, only the reasons for the fortune are different.

It's not the girls who go for that face, it's the boys. And take a look at that face, a close look. It's pinched, tired and lined as if he has all the worries in the world.

But it's his fortune.

"Only about 40 per cent. of my fans are girls," reveals Gene in a voice so quiet that it's barely audible. "But it's better this way. I don't get all that screaming, and I don't make the boys jealous."

That is a long sentence for Gene. He's moody, quiet, appears to be shy and is quite happy to let someone else do the talking for him. He registers no change of expression when his name is mentioned and rarely smiles.

There's a slight trace of a grin however, when the subject of his face comes up. But he doesn't say much about it. "No, I guess it isn't very beautiful, but I wouldn't change it."

Says his road manager, "The fans all look upon Gene as being one of them. They turn up at the stage door sometimes in their hundreds all wearing black leather outfits the same as Gene wears on stage.

"They crack jokes with him, asking where he's left his motor bike, and all seem to like him. Not once have we had any rowdyism or trouble.

THE 'TOUGHS' HAVE CHANGED

"Sometimes they have even helped us to clear a way for Gene to get to the car. And these are the real toughs who usually make trouble for other stars."

When his friend, Eddie Cochran was killed in that tragic car crash last April, Gene suffered a great personal loss.

He felt incredibly lonely, and his loneliness made him feel even more homesick.

Then came the news about his daughter and his hurried return home. Gene Vincent certainly has had it hard.

But though Eddie's death first brought on this loneliness it also helped in one small way to make life a little easier. With Gene's consent his road manager says: "Ever since Eddie's death the fans have been far more considerate to Gene.

"At one time when Eddie and Gene were touring together there used to be massive crowds outside the stage door who just wouldn't let either of them through. Now the same crowds are there, but they're far more considerate to Gene. They still seem to sense that he has lost a friend and try to help him."

Says Gene: "I guess they feel sorry for me."

He seems to be miles away as he says this, but no more sad than he usually looks. I ask his manager how he tells whether Gene is sad or not.

I'm told: "It takes a long time and you have to know him very well before you can tell . . ."

The one thing which Gene shows any real enthusiasm for is his new record "Pistol Packin' Mama," arranged for him by Eddie just before he died, and "Weeping Willow."

He plays me the disc and asks whether I like it or not. I say I do.

But I couldn't tell whether my comment made him happy or not.

It would have done, I think, if it hadn't been for those tragedies.

All about Eddie

IT'S happened again. One of the world's best rock singers killed in a car crash. It was only recently that Eddie Cochran was becoming more popular in England, due to his tour and several appearances in "Boy Meets Girls."

I was a great fan of his since I saw him in "The Girl Can't Help It" in 1957 and hearing him sing "20 Flight Rock." I saw the film seven times simply because Eddie was in it.

I write on behalf of all his fans when I say we will all miss him terribly. He was a great singer who will be remembered for a long time to come.—DIANE LORD, 65, Middlecotes, Tile Hill Lane, Coventry.

WHAT a great loss Eddie Cochran is to the rock world. Eddie may be gone, but his style of music will continue to live on in the hearts of the people who understand and appreciate rock as only he could sing it.

As I see it, only Elvis continues above all to carry the golden banner of rock and the big beat.—CRAIG SCOTT, 34, Cromwell Road, Derby.

IT was with very deep regret that I read of Eddie Cochran's tragic death. I found Eddie to be completely unspoiled by success and very excited about being in England and meeting the people who bought his records.

Now he is no longer with us, but he has left a fine collection of records behind that will continue to give much pleasure to rock fans old and new.

I am sure I speak for all his fans in saying that his name will be remembered with loyalty and sincerity. — ALEX GORDON, 50, Central Avenue, Kilbirnie, Ayrshire, Scotland.

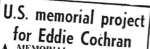

U.S. memorial project for Eddie Cochran

A MEMORIAL concert for Eddie Cochran is planned by U.S. impresario Norm Riley, the man who set up the singer-guitarist's British tour. It will be held in the vast El Monte Legion Stadium, California, close to Cochran's home and the scene of his first professional engagement.

Duane Eddy and Johnny and The Hurricanes have already offered their services if a suitable date can be found. When Riley leaves London on May 8 he will fly to California to set up a date for the concert, probably in June.

Cochran was buried at a private ceremony at Forest Lawns Cemetery, Glendale, California, on Monday. Only close members of his family and a few friends were present.

Decca are bringing out " Three Steps To Heaven," the record Eddie Cochran was returning to America to launch when he was involved in the fatal accident, next Friday (6th). It will be coupled with " Cut Across Shorty."

GENE VINCENT (left) and JERRY KELLER arrived at London airport on Friday for the tour in which Keller is to take the place of Eddie Cochran.

123

10. AND THE NIGHT IS SO LONELY
Repercussions

"How long have you been on the road?"
"All my life."
(BBC radio interview with Gene Vincent, 1971)

The story of Eddie and Gene had had an unexpected ending as it appeared to be Gene who was heading for destruction, not Eddie, so in many ways, the least likely person died. However, the accident took its toll of Gene and something in him died as well. For the last 10 years of his life, he was a hollow shell.

Gene Vincent's dates in Paris in April 1960 were cancelled. He flew to New York and was reunited with his wife, Darlene. They went to Hazel Dell, Vancouver to stay with Darlene's family and to escape the media, who had no idea where he was.

A businessman first and foremost, Larry Parnes had no intention of cancelling the second leg of the UK tour. Rather than being sympathetic, he was furious with Gene and Eddie for taking a taxi that night. Gene Vincent had a contract and he would do the shows as arranged and Parnes brought in Jerry Keller of 'Here Comes Summer' fame to replace Eddie Cochran on the tour. Apart from 'Here Comes Summer', the Arkansas balladeer had little to offer, but he did his best. Realising that a Gene Vincent audience wanted rock'n'roll, he expanded his range, jumping on the piano for one song and then leaping into the footlights. No one was impressed, but at least he was trying. Possibly Ronnie Hawkins, another of Norm Riley's artists, would have been more suitable. Gene was being paid $2,240 a week for the tour, most of it landing in Norm Riley's pocket.

Adrian Owlett: "Gene came back to England shortly after the crash with Darlene but she didn't stay long. Today, singers cancel gigs for sore throats but Gene was back on stage even though he'd been through that crash and was suffering from severe stress and anguish. He was strapped up in bandages but you could never have guessed from the way he performed that he was so ill." Gene Vincent found the tour very difficult. He was under immense stress and he would say, "And now I want to sing to you Eddie's favourite song", which was a cue for 'Over The Rainbow'.

Gene worked again with the Beat Boys, and Keller used Nero and the Gladiators. Their leader, Mike O'Neill, from Bolton would say, "I come to dig Caesar not to bury him" and their instrumentals included a rock version of 'In The Hall Of The Mountain King'. Dave Dover recalls seeing the band at the Cavern: "Nero and the Gladiators were dressed like Roman centurions but their skirts looked like the blinds that you buy for your windows. The bass player wiggled his hips and moved from side to side. When the

Beatles came on, McCartney was skitting him and he got it totally right. He did his act and the whole of the Cavern was in bulk as this guy had looked so stupid. The Beatles were brilliant but that band was awful." There was no need for these ersatz Gladiators as there was something about the real gladiatorial appearance in Gene himself.

The usual suspects *sans* Vince Eager were in support: Lance Fortune, the Viscounts, Peter Wynne and Georgie Fame as well as Vince Taylor (an American from Hounslow who aped Presley) and Davy Jones (the singer who befriended the Beatles in Hamburg, not the Monkee). Other acts came and went – Billy Fury, Joe Brown, Michael Cox, Duffy Power, Dickie Pride and Sally Kelly.

The tour began with a fortnight of one-nighters, starting at the Gaumont, Hanley on 30 April 1960. While the Eddie and Gene tour was in Liverpool, Parnes had met a local entrepreneur, Allan Williams, who had suggested a rock'n'roll festival at Liverpool Stadium on May 3. The original flyer referred to "The return of Eddie Cochran" and it would have been sensational if Williams had pulled it off.

"I was shattered by the death of Eddie Cochran," says Allan Williams, "Gene Vincent was also badly hurt and I phoned Larry Parnes about a week later and said, 'I take it for granted that it's all over.' He said, 'No. Gene Vincent has gone back to the States but he's returning to England and would like to do it.' So I thought I'd put on Liverpool groups to supplement the show - Rory Storm and the Hurricanes, Bob Evans and the Five Shillings, and Cass and the Cassanovas. Bob Wooler came to the Jacaranda and suggested I have Gerry and the Pacemakers. I went along to Blair Hall and was knocked out by them, and so we went ahead with the first ever Merseybeat/ rock 'n' roll show." The event prompted Parnes to come to Liverpool with Billy Fury a week later to see if there was a suitable backing group for him. That didn't work out but Parnes did sign the fledgling Beatles to back Johnny Gentle on a short tour of Scotland.

The Beatles weren't considered good enough to be included. Perhaps it was just as well. John Gustafson was playing with Cass and the Cassanovas: "Larry Parnes was at the stadium and he saw me and thought, 'Star quality', or something like that. He took me to London and I did a recording test in Denmark Street which was a shambles, me singing 'Money Honey' on an electric guitar, which was not even plugged in. (Laughs) He treated me very well, but I was very wary about him - my dad had given me a lecture before I went. He bought me some clothes and I was a 17-year-old being showered with gifts. Things turned sour because I didn't go along with his grand plan. I returned to Liverpool and carried on as before."

Back to the Gene Vincent tour: Lance Fortune: "There was never enough security at the concerts. No one would stop the Teddy Boys from getting up on stage. I remember them getting up at Northampton but they weren't being threatening. They just formed a circle round Gene and it was like he was in the middle of a hokey-cokey."

Gene's UK fan club secretary, Alan Vince, found Gene introspective and moody and he was passing time by throwing a knife at the dressing-room door. Jerry Keller said, "You want me to write an article for the fan club? I'll tell you a few stories about this guy." "Okay," said Gene, "I know I'm no angel."

Ray McVay: "Gene was a nasty character and I kept clear of him if I could. He drank very heavily and he had a terrible grudge against everyone. He hated to see us jumping around and doing things because he was lumbered with his bad leg. When he came back after Eddie's death, he was worse than ever. He didn't know what the hell was going on."

Vincent's behaviour was becoming even more manic. He was always creating tension and asking other performers if they wanted to meet Henry. Henry was his knife. One night on the tour bus, he cut Hal Carter's clothes to shreds while he was wearing them. Joe Brown: "I can remember Gene sitting in the front of the coach, sharpening his knife. He then leapt up and said to Hal Carter, 'I'm gonna cut you in 14 places.' Swish, swish, swish. That was the end of Hal's suit."

Johnny Gentle: "He pulled a knife on us in the coach once. He thought we were all laughing about him."

On May 11, Gene recorded a new single at EMI, a revival of the Andrews Sisters' "Pistol Packin' Mama', produced by Norrie Paramor. Eddie had worked out the arrangement for Gene and they followed his blueprint with Georgie Fame on piano. No doubt a song about guns had appealed to both Gene and Eddie. The B-side was a dark and touching ballad, 'Weeping Willow', written by Gene under a pseudonym.

> *"I've lost my love, you've lost your love,*
> *Why do you weep, dear willow,*
> *'Cause that's why your branches hang so low."*

Gene was in a volatile mood when he made the record. He went berserk when a take went wrong but the next moment it was back to "Yes, Mr Paramor, sir."

Georgie Fame: "Gene was a bit moody but he was very nice to me 'cause I was young and green. I've got a photograph of him and me together and also a signed photograph which says, 'To Georgie, Thanks for covering all my mistakes, Gene Vincent'. The very first recording I was involved with was a single that he cut in London of 'Pistol Packin' Mama'. It was me on piano, the original Blue Flames and four string players, and I was 16 at the time."

'Three Steps To Heaven' entered the charts on 12 May 1960 and climbed to No.1. It turned out that there was far more in the vaults than Liberty had revealed and over the coming months, Eddie made the charts with

'Weekend' and 'Jeannie, Jeannie, Jeannie' as well as 'The Eddie Cochran Memorial Album'.

With the commercial success of 'Three Steps To Heaven', Parnes decided to turn the tour into 'The Eddie Cochran Tribute Show'. In its new guise, the tour would begin with a week at the Glasgow Empire on 6 June 1960. As well as Vincent, there would be Joe Brown, Billy Fury, Lance Fortune and Georgie Fame and each act would do a number associated with Cochran. Billy Raymond would be the compère. Parnes announced that part of the proceeds would go to Cochran's family.

The bizarre event included Billy Fury introducing Sharon Sheeley, who was still suffering from a fractured neck and back. She wanted to make it up to Gene but when she went to his dressing room, she heard him say, "Well, do you think I should wear the black leathers, Ed, or should I wear this blue shirt?" Sharon found it too ghoulish and quit after a couple of days. By now, Gene had his tartan suit which he wore from time to time. Also, the rockers at the Glasgow Empire still had no love for Billy Fury. Missiles flew and things got so out of hand one night that seven theatregoers were arrested.

Hal Carter: "Gene did try and kill himself. Once it was with drink and pills and once he gave himself a number of cuts: he may have cut his wrists, I can't remember. He got stranger and stranger on that tour and I passed him over to Peter Grant. Gene was scared stiff of Peter so that made him behave. Peter would grab him by the neck and fling him against the wall." The shrewd and ruthless Grant was to make his reputation as the manager of Led Zeppelin.

The tour moved to the Theatre Royal, Nottingham. Gene told the audience that he had a telegram from Darlene stating that his young daughter, Melody, had died of pneumonia. The tears streamed down Gene's face. Gene cancelled his appearances in Liverpool, Birmingham and Cardiff as well as a summer season in Blackpool. Sharon sent him a note telling him how sad she felt for him.

Gene returned home but there was nothing wrong with Melody, and the telegram was a hoax. The suspicion, never proved, was that Gene had sent the telegram to himself (if indeed there ever was a telegram). Of course it was a hoax and of course Gene had sent it to himself. He was desperate to get out of his tour and he had such a twisted mind that it was quite in keeping with his behaviour. If he had not sent the telegram himself and thought it was genuine, what would he have done? The answer, quite simply, is ring Darlene. He was calling her all the time anyway, and he would have found out that the telegram was false. The press wanted to contact Gene, but he had disappeared and was possibly staying with Darlene's parents in Canada. Gene's biographer, Rob Finnis: "The telegram was completely fabricated by Gene and I don't know anybody who ever saw it. When he went on stage, he mumbled what he was going to say. The audience thought he was talking about his dog, Melody, instead of his daughter, Melody. They were laughing at first and then they started crying. He was pleased with the reaction and he told the next audience about Melody and the next and the next and then he went home. Only a nutter could have made up something as outrageous as that, and I can't believe that Darlene went along with it. His relationship with Darlene didn't last much longer and when Parnes found out the telegram was false, he dropped Gene completely. Gene was always screwing it up with people and then getting away from them. He would find a new set of people to work with and that would work well at first because of his reputation. Then he would blow that too. The reason he came to England was because he had run out of options in the States."

Parnes was furious, threatening Vincent with legal action and saying, "Certainly the cancellation put us to a lot of trouble in rearranging acts." His manager, Norm Riley, was equally disappointed but when he said that Vincent was mentally ill, Parnes backtracked. Parnes concluded, "I am not taking any action. Any damage that has been done, Vincent has done to himself." He had had his fill of American stars and in a typical *volte-face*, he declared in 'Disc' in July 1960, "Apart from Elvis Presley, I don't think there's a single American singer the public wants to see. You see, our boys have got the experience behind them before they step out on to the stage." What Parnes didn't know is that he just had the Beatles in his hands and let them go.

That aside, Parnes was in a particularly buoyant mood. In July 1960 a Scottish businessman Huw McCowan paid £100,000 for a half-share in Parnes's business. And quite possibly, Vincent's extraordinary behaviour gave Norm Riley a few ideas of his own. In a couple of years' time when his artists were chasing him for their money, he committed himself to an asylum and stayed there until the heat wore off.

Parnes' deal with Fielding and Bevan for Marty Wilde's services had not worked out as well as expected. The contract was terminated in July 1960 and Marty starred in a summer season at Bournemouth. He was still performing rock'n'roll with the Wildcats but his set also included a stunning version of Julie London's 'Cry Me A River' and the Platters' 'My Prayer'. In October, however, he stood in for Billy Fury and Joe Brown, who both had influenza, at the Free Trade Hall in Manchester and was booed by angry teenagers. In 1961, he appeared in the film, 'The Hellions', and made his West End debut, very successfully, in the rock'n'roll spoof, 'Bye Bye Birdie'.

Considering that Tony Sheridan was such a feral beast in Hamburg during the Beatles' time in Hamburg, I am surprised that he was so docile during the Cochran tour and its aftermath. It is probably because he was the opening act and he was overawed by the American performers. At the start of 1961, he was hired to play at the Top Ten Club in Hamburg and from there, he went to the Star-Club. He had three reasons to leave the UK: Parnes, who prided punctuality and obedience above everything, was finding him unreliable; he had signed a hire purchase agreement for his Martin guitar under a false name; and he had made a girlfriend pregnant. He needed to make a new start and indeed, when he did eventually return to the UK, he was arrested for fraud and spent ten days in prison.

Gene Vincent spent the summer with Darlene and the children in Oregon. While he was away from the UK, he had two successes, 'Pistol Packin' Mama' made No.15 and the 'Crazy Times' LP made No.12 on the album charts.

Don Arden had been the MC on Gene Vincent's first UK tour for Larry Parnes. He realised that promoting your own shows could be lucrative. He began with a few rock'n'roll packages in north London dance halls and then, starting in 1961, he brought over Gene Vincent. A tough man himself, he thought he could deal with Vincent's wayward behaviour and he knew that Vincent would back down once you stood up to him. Not, however, that the tours were without incident. On 14 June 1961, Vincent fell down 30 steps after coming off stage at the Newcastle Majestic and was knocked unconscious. His bad leg was further damaged in the accident and several dates were cancelled.

Chas Hodges, then with the Outlaws: "Don Arden treated Gene like a child. He had to. You couldn't take your eyes off him for two seconds. If you turned your back on him, he would go straight into a bar and drink five Scotches on the trot. I think he used his bad leg to play on people's sympathies. We used to say, 'Oh, shut up, you're all right" and he'd go quiet. Treat him as one of the boys and he'd be okay. Whenever Don Arden was around, he would really play it up."

Alan Holmes, who backed him in Sounds Incorporated: "Gene was a lunatic on stage. He nearly killed us several times with the mike stands. We learnt to get out of his way. He also used the mike stand as a crutch and even though he had a bad leg, there would be a lot of movement. He'd be kneeling down a lot of the time. We didn't know in what order he would do the songs. He'd say, 'Give me an E, John' and we'd have to follow him."

Wes Hunter, also from Sounds Inc: "He wore the same black leather suit for every appearance. He never had it cleaned and it was pretty high by the end of a tour. A lot of his fans would have worn leather suits as well but they were pretty expensive at the time."

Alan Holmes: "Gene used to wear those American bomber jackets, a bit like something out of 'Happy Days'. You see them all the time now but they were very unusual in England then. He lost a lot of clothes though. He used to wander off from hotels without them and he often left money on the mantelpiece."

Road manager Henry Henroid: "Gene had very few possessions. He was the original vagabond. He took a case on tour with him and there was hardly anything in it. It never occurred to him to have his black leather suit cleaned. He was clean in some respects in that he took a lot of baths but I never saw him clean his teeth. He once put razor blades in my soap. He did it just because I had given him a bollocking. I saw the blades before I used the soap and I went and gave him another one."

In July 1961, Vincent starred for a week at the Bristol Hippodrome. Revisiting the theatre was an eerie experience for him. When someone knocked on his dressing-room door, he said, "Tell Eddie I'll be right out." When they drove away after the engagement, Vincent was huddled in his seat, refusing to look out of the window. Wes Hunter: "We did a show in Bristol with Gene and I was driving a hired car back to London. I almost came a cropper at the same bend that Eddie died, and Gene was in the back, absolutely petrified."

In 1964, Gene pulled himself together for a Granada TV special, 'Whole Lotta Shakin' Goin' On' with Jerry Lee Lewis, produced by Johnny Hamp. "I'm so glad that we made that programme in black and white as Gene was made for black and white. He looked superb with the spotlight hitting him and you can see the gloss on his leathers." The film has a slow-moving tracking shot down Gene Vincent's bad leg, a bizarre touch in a world of perfectly formed singers.

Gene's life became a series of tragic incidents, both privately and professionally. He would have mock suicides and he lived in an alcoholic haze. He could still cut it when he wanted to, but he didn't want to very often. Derek Johnson of the NME: "I met Gene about three years after the crash. He was looking at the charts and he said, 'Look at what Elvis is recording now. Eddie would have overtaken him if he'd been alive.'"

Mick O'Toole: "I saw Gene Vincent at the Locarno in Liverpool in 1964. Two guys led him on to the stage, took him to the microphone, placed it in his hands and went away. He was in that classic pose where nobody knew what he was looking at and he seemed to be ignoring the crowd completely. He seemed totally out of it, completely gone. Vocally, he was very good indeed and at the end, the same two guys came and led him away. I bet if I had stopped him and asked him where he was, he wouldn't have had a clue." There were plenty of Eddie Cochran tracks to be released and he had a Top 20 hit with 'Weekend' in 1961. The B-side was Sharon Sheeley's song 'Cherished Memories', which sounded doubly poignant now. Eddie was also the subject of Heinz's 1963 Top 5 hit, 'Just Like Eddie', which was produced by Joe Meek. Heinz said, "Many a time people have said to me, 'Is that record about Duane Eddy?', but it should have been obvious with 'C'mon Everybody' in there. Eddie was my idol - Elvis, Buddy Holly, Gene Vincent and Jerry Lee Lewis were great but there's only one rock'n'roller for me. That's why I loved the song so much. Eddie is so underrated and I like to keep his legend alive and remind people that he was a great man, a fantastic artist." Also by way of a tribute to Eddie, Michael Cox and the Wildcats recorded 'Sweet Little Sixteen' in Eddie's arrangement and Joe Brown used the same arrangement on stage.

Dave Dee was with Gene in the week before he died. "In 1971 we were playing at the Shakespeare in Liverpool and Gene was at the Wooky Hollow. Just by chance we were in the same digs in Leigh. He was well gone by then, but he wasn't too bad when I went to see him on the first night. However, after the second night, he got paid off and I remember him coming back, full of tears. A couple of days later, he was dead."

Gene Vincent died on 12 October 1971, officially following the complications of a burst ulcer but it was much more than that. He was a destitute, confused, overweight, alcoholic, humiliated wreck. He had become a Buddhist, though he had little concept as to what this entailed. Having been a marine, he often said that he wanted to be buried at sea. On 15 October, his mother gave him a standard Christian burial. He was buried in his black leathers at Eternal Valley Memorial Park in Newhall, California. After 15 nomadic years, Gene Vincent was staying put.

**GENE VINCENT — Walkin'
Home From School; I Got A Baby**
(Capitol CL14830).
In the usual Vincent tradition, it
rocks from start to finish and you
can't understand a word! Fine for
dancing.

**GENE VINCENT
Baby Blue; True To You**
(Capitol C114868)✱✱✱
ROCK 'N' ROLLER Gene
Vincent has just appeared in
the film "Hot Rod Gang"—and
for the screen he sings **Baby Blue**.
It's a heavy beater, one of his own
compositions.
Routine rocker, I'm afraid,
despite all the frantic effort Gene
puts into it.
I prefer the beat-ballad **True To
You** which comes up on the flip.
Gene and his Blue Caps trot
through this one with a certain
amount of infectious charm. A
likeable half.

**GENE VINCENT
Say Mama: Be Bop Boogie Boy**
(Capitol CL 14974)✱✱✱
GENE VINCENT is another
rock star who has never
realised his full potential on this
side of the sea.
But he has a strong beat number
in **Say Mama**. Chants it in lively
fashion while the Blue Caps give
him a thudding background.
There's also some energetic saxophone added to their noise this
time.
Gene gets composer credit for
the song on the second side. **Be
Bop Boogie Boy** is another bound-
ing rock 'n' roller. Boogie in the
beat with just the right sort of
clinking piano brought in to provide the atmosphere it needs.

DISC
THE TOP RECORD & MUSICAL WEEKLY

EVERY 6D THURSDAY

GENE VINCENT

No. 25   Week ending, August 16, 1958

001...001...001...

★ Another Eddie Cochran disc

A record the late **Eddie Cochran** made for Liberty Records before he died has been released this week and has received excellent reviews. Best side is a rock-a-billy type song called "Sweety Pie," which is backed by a rock ballad, "Lonely."

The lyrics sound strange now, but EDDIE COCHRAN had a winner with "Lonely" (DISC Pic).

GENE VINCENT
Crazy Times
Crazy Times; She She Little Sheila; Darlene; Everybody's Got A Date But Me; Why Don't You People Learn How To Drive; Green Back Dollar; Big Fat Saturday Night; Michiko From Tokyo; Hot Dollar; Accentuate The Positive; Blue Eyes Crying In The Rain; Pretty Pearly.

(Capitol T.1342)★★★★

THIS is one of the best albums to come from Gene Vincent yet and I know that it is going to prove a big seller. I must admit he is not my cup of tea, but he serves up the typical excitement which appeals to today's younger record customers and that is the secret of success.

The album is full of those beaty rhythms and staccato lyrics which the teenagers feel they could perform themselves—and probably could.

Nothing else for me to say about this one except that if you are a rock enthusiast then this is right up your street.

EDDIE COCHRAN
Lonely; Sweetie Pie
(London HLG9196)

ONE or two lines in "Lonely" strike strangely to the ear—particularly when the late Eddie Cochran sings that he wishes he could die! But this is a beater which has the mark of a big seller all right. Eddie put it over in deep tones with vocal group and rhythm behind him. Cannot see it missing the parade.

"Sweetie Pie" is a quicker, happier rocker which had Cochran in good form again. Guitar noise and rattling sticks behind him as he trots through this one.

GENE VINCENT AND EDDIE COCHRAN IN THE UK

Transmission dates are shown.

Television:

'Boy Meets Girls' (ABC TV)

12.12.59
'Bluejean Bop', 'Five Days, Five Days', 'Say Mama' (all abridged) – Gene Vincent
'Be Bop A Lula' – Gene Vincent (Rebel Heart, Volume 4, Magnum Force CDMF 097, 1997)

19.12.59 (recorded 11.12.59)
'Rocky Road Blues' – Gene Vincent
'Frankie And Johnny' – Gene Vincent
'Wild Cat' – Gene Vincent
'Right Here On Earth' – Gene Vincent
All recordings are on 'Rebel Heart, Volume 5', Magnum Force CDMF 099, 1998.

26.12.59 (recorded 11.12.59)
'Baby Blue' – Gene Vincent
'I Got A Baby' – Gene Vincent
'Summertime' – Gene Vincent
'Right Here On Earth' – Gene Vincent

16.1.60
* 'Hallelujah I Love Her So' – Eddie Cochran
* 'C'mon Everybody'- Eddie Cochran
* 'Somethin' Else' – Eddie Cochran
* 'Twenty Flight Rock' – Eddie Cochran

23.1.60 (recorded 15.1.60)
* 'Money Honey' – Eddie Cochran
* 'Have I Told You Lately That I Love You' – Eddie Cochran
* 'Hallelujah I Love Her So' – Eddie Cochran

20.2.60 (recorded 19.2.60)
'Say Mama', **'Wild Cat' and 'Be Bop A Lula' (all abridged) – Gene Vincent
'Hallelujah I Love Her So' and 'Twenty Flight Rock' (both abridged) –

Eddie Cochran
* 'Summertime Blues' – Eddie Cochran
* 'Milk Cow Blues' – Eddie Cochran
'My Heart' – Gene Vincent (Eddie Cochran, lead guitar)
*** 'Dance In The Street' – Gene Vincent (Eddie Cochran, lead guitar)
**** 'My Babe' – Gene Vincent, Marty Wilde and Billy Fury (vocals) and Eddie Cochran (vocals and lead guitar)

27.2.60 (recorded 19.2.60)
* 'I Don't Like You No More' – Eddie Cochran
* 'Sweet Little Sixteen' – Eddie Cochran
'My Heart' – Gene Vincent (Eddie Cochran, lead guitar)
'I've Got To Get You Yet' – Gene Vincent
* 'White Lightnin'' – Gene Vincent (vocal) and Eddie Cochran (vocal, lead guitar)

* 'Rock'n'Roll Memories – Eddie Cochran and Gene Vincent', Rockstar RSRCD 018, 2000
** 'Sweet Gene Vincent', OZit Morpheus CD 221, 2004
*** Gene Vincent LP, 'Rareties (sic), Volume 2', Doktor Collector CK 005, France, 1985.
**** Billy Fury CD, 'Rarities And Teenager Jottings', OZit Morpheus, CD 233, 2004

Musicians on 'Boy Meets Girls' were Joe Brown, Eric Ford, Brian Daly (guitars), Red Price (tenor sax), Cherry Wainer (organ), Bill Stark (double-bass), Alan Weighell (electric bass), Andy White, Don Storer (drums) and the Vernons Girls. Brass and strings added on occasion.

'Lunch Box' (ATV, Birmingham)

12.3.60
Eddie Cochran and Gene Vincent: details unknown.

Radio:

'Parade Of The Pops' (BBC Light Programme)

15.2.60
Wildcat – Gene Vincent
My Heart – Gene Vincent

22.2.60
Hallelujah I Love Her So – Eddie Cochran
*C'mon Everybody – Eddie Cochran

Both acts were accompanied by Bob Miller and the Millermen.

'Saturday Club' (BBC Light Programme)

5.3.60 (probably recorded 23.2.60)
** 'Say Mama' – Gene Vincent
** 'Summertime' – Gene Vincent
** 'Somethin' Else' – Eddie Cochran
** 'Hallelujah I Love Her So' – Eddie Cochran
** 'Be Bop A Lula'– Gene Vincent
*/** 'Twenty Flight Rock'– Eddie Cochran
** 'Rocky Road Blues' – Gene Vincent
** 'C'mon Everybody' – Eddie Cochran

12.3.60 (probably recorded 23.2.60)
** 'Wild Cat' – Gene Vincent
** 'My Heart' – Gene Vincent (Eddie Cochran, lead guitar)
* 'Say Mama' – Gene Vincent
* 'Be Bop A Lula'– Gene Vincent
** 'What'd I Say'– Eddie Cochran
** 'Milk Cow Blues'– Eddie Cochran

The initial contracts for 'Saturday Club' show that the recordings would be at 7pm on 16 February 1960. However, the running order for the two shows gives a recording date of 23 February 1960. The likelihood is that there was a last minute switch and the recordings were on the later date.

Musicians on 'Saturday Club' were Jim Sullivan (lead guitar), Tony Belcher (rhythm guitar), Brian Locking (bass) and Brian Bennett (drums).

Recorded Interviews:

Gene Vincent with Brian Matthew (Saturday Club, BBC, 5.12.59)
* Gene Vincent with Ray Orchard (Recorded at London Airport, 5.12.59 for transmission on Capitol Show, Radio Luxembourg, 11.12.59: on CD, 'Blue 'Gene' Bop', Rockstar RSRCD 025, 2005)
* Eddie Cochran with unknown interviewer (Gaumont, Ipswich, 24.1.60: on album, 'The Legendary Eddie Cochran', United Artists UAS 29163, 1971)
Gene Vincent and Eddie Cochran with Monty Lister (Radio interview for

Clatterbridge and Cleaver Hospitals on the Wirral, probably 15 March 1960: on CD, 'Rock'n'Roll Memories', Rockstar RSRCD 018, 2000)

* 'On Tour With Gene And Eddie', Rockstar RSR EP 2013, 1986 (7-inch EP)
** 'Rock'n'Roll Memories – Eddie Cochran and Gene Vincent', Rockstar RSRCD 018, 2000

BIBLIOGRAPHY

Wild Cat: A Tribute To Gene Vincent – Edited by Eddie Muir (Self-published, 1977)

Somethin' Else; A Tribute To Eddie Cochran – Edited by Eddie Muir and Tony Scott (VRRAS, 1979)
Both contain press cuttings with short features

Gene Vincent Story, 1956 – Gerard Lautrey and Serge Schlawick (Crazy Times Revue, 1978)
Gene Vincent Story, 1957-58 – Gerard Lautrey and Serge Schlawick (Crazy Times Revue, 1979)
Gene Vincent Story, 1959-60– Gerard Lautrey and Serge Schlawick (Crazy Times Revue, 1980)
Largely press cuttings and photographs with French text. Two later volumes.

The Day The World Turned Blue: A Biography Of Gene Vincent – Britt Hagarty (Blandford, 1984)
Plenty of excellent detail and well written.

Gene Vincent: The Story Behind His Songs – Thierry Liesenfeld (Blue Gene Bop, 1992)
600 A4 pages – the lyrics of all Gene's songs with recording details and cover versions.

Three Steps To Heaven – John Firminger (Self-published, 1998)
Press cuttings and story of the 1960 tour

Sweet Gene Vincent: The Bitter End – Steven Mandich (Orange Syringe, 1999)
Some good features but a bit wayward as a biography

Race With The Devil: Gene Vincent's Life In The Fast Lane – Susan Van Hecke (St Martin's Press, 2000)
Established author, great story, but sloppily written.

Don't Forget Me: The Eddie Cochran Story – Julie Mundy and Darrel Higham (Mainstream, 2000)
Darrel, an excellent rockabilly performer, was so excited when he was writing this book that I thought it was going to be a definitive work. It isn't, largely because the publishers wouldn't allow it to be long enough.

American Rock'n'Roll: The UK Tours, 1956-72 – Ian Wallis (Music Mentor, 2003)
Complete tour listings for the US performers who played the UK in the early years. With contemporary reviews and details of supporting acts, this is a very useful research tool and it is also a great read. Who else but Gene Vincent for the cover, the US star who performed the most in the UK?

Three Steps To Heaven: The Eddie Cochran Story – Bobby Cochran with Susan Van Hecke (Hal Leonard, 2003)
Cochran is a competent musician himself (ex-Steppenwolf) and has played and recorded his uncle's songs. He was only 10 when Eddie died and though he knew the main participants, there are too many factual errors to sound convincing.

Gene Vincent And Eddie Cochran: Rock'n'Roll Revolutionaries – John Collis (Virgin, 2004)
Good book, good author but why tell the story out of sequence?

Gene Vincent: There's One In Every Town – Mick Farren (Do Not Press, 2004)
Short memoir with thought-provoking assessments: "If rock was literature, he'd probably have been Jean Genet."

Gene Vincent: A Companion – Derek Henderson (Spent Brothers, 2005)
Superbly comprehensive discography but can be hard to follow, largely because there are so many versions of the same song. Still, Gene Vincent completists will want all 43 versions of 'Be Bop A Lula'.